RELAPSE

Biblical Prevention Strategies

MARK E. SHAW

Endorsements

"Relapse is a valuable tool for the Christian who has experienced the grace of the gospel, but finds himself drawn back to captivating sins. Shaw's big picture answer is knowing and trusting God. What this workbook does is provide tools for deepening faith and confidence in God. This is a valuable tool for counselors."

Dr. Tedd Tripp, Pastor, Conference speaker, and
Author of *Shepherding a Child's Heart*

"Mark Shaw has done all of us who minister to men and women trapped in the addictions of sin a great service. With biblical fidelity and practical clarity he has not only reminded us that addictions are rooted in sinful choices, but that sinful choices are the result of a sin nature enticed by a love of the world that enslaves and destroys instead of the love of Christ that redeems and renews. Mark has wonderfully and insightfully displayed how the glorious Gospel of Jesus Christ takes sinners who come to Christ "just as I am," yet will not leave them where He saved them but both freely forgives and gloriously transforms so that the redeemed might know Him and display Him with the joy of forgiveness and the exhilaration of glorifying God and enjoying Him forever. In a word from the Word: "The wages of sin is death, BUT the free gift of God is eternal life through Christ our Lord" (Romans 6:23)."

Harry L. Reeder III, Senior Pastor
Briarwood Presbyterian Church
Birmingham, Alabama

"I am honored to endorse, *Relapse*, Mark Shaw's latest in his series of books on addictions. The Lovelady Center is a transitional facility for troubled women who have struggled with all kinds of trials in overcoming their personal addictions. For years we searched for the best curriculum we could find with which to teach our women. We are now firmly grounded with his books. He has a gift and a passion for speaking the truth of God's Word in the love of the Holy Spirit to all those he comes in contact here with our 400+ women, or in the context of the biblical counseling he offers at local churches all over the greater Birmingham area. Mark has a simple, purely biblical way of teaching and encouraging in love that few possess, and he's able to pull off telling people the hardest of truths and lead them to experience the love of the Holy Spirit in such a way that they keep coming back for more. If you want to understand the BIG truths of God's Word as they relate to your seemingly insurmountable problem of addiction, then read *Relapse* and ALL of Mark's books on addiction. He gives down to earth, practical explanations of the problem from God's perspective revealed in His Word. With the forgiveness of sins from Jesus Christ and the Holy Spirit's power which comes to all who believe in Him, all can be transformed to overcome any addiction for the glory of God."

Brenda Lovelady, Founder and Executive Director
Lovelady Center, Birmingham, AL

"For too long, Christians have been leaning on the broken-reed teachings of psychotherapy to find answers to their problems. The best these 'experts' can offer the struggling addict is to label his behavior a disease and attempt to curb that which they cannot cure. How refreshing then is Dr. Mark Shaw's most recent book, *Relapse: Biblical Prevention Strategies*, in which he leads his readers down the 'ancient paths' of biblical wisdom. By calling addictive behavior SIN, he directs the addict to the one solution that actually works: a right relationship with Jesus Christ."

Steve Gallagher, Founder, Pure Life Ministries

"I am grateful for Mark Shaw. Whether writing a book or in a one-on-one conversation with an individual, Mark is committed to biblically rooted and God-glorifying counsel. Mark is not interested in behavior modification, but gospel transformation."

David Nasser, Lead Pastor
Christ City Church, Birmingham, AL

"Mark's book *Relapse: Biblical Prevention Strategies* is a unique and valuable resource that our network of "Christ" centered addiction support groups can utilize while embracing struggling individuals with the hope of the gospel. It clearly points out that we are without excuse and can no longer claim ignorance. It's practical, hands-on, rubber-meets-the–road approach of unpacking biblical truths will provide much needed Godly perspective pertaining to the relapse cycle. I'm confident that the Holy Spirit will use this and Mark's many other addiction related materials to better equip the church; and help many brokenhearted individuals and their loved ones into a deeper walk with Christ Jesus, and into a more firm connection with their local church."

Daniel & Rosemary Gavin, Addictions Victorious, Deptford, NJ
www.AddVicInc.org

"In an age in which the therapeutic reigns, even inside the church, Mark Shaw provides a cure for addiction and relapse that is as time-tested as the problem itself: God's word. Unflinchingly biblical and utterly Gospel-centered, Relapse provides a life-altering solution to a deep and abiding problem and shows that, contrary to the alleged wisdom of popular psychology, the enemy is not outside of us but inside, and the cure is not inside us, but outside us, in the grace and mercy of our Lord Jesus Christ. If you have relapsed into addiction or know someone who is wrestling with this debilitating issue, read this book and be prepared to be transformed by the grace of a merciful God."

Jeff Robinson, Ph.D., The Southern Baptist Theological Seminary
Pastor, Philadelphia Baptist Church, Birmingham, Alabama
Senior editor, The Council on Biblical Manhood and Womanhood

"Relapse! Ah, what an awful word for the individual and the family of the "addict." Mark Shaw takes on the challenge both of prevention and biblical recovery. This is more than a workbook. It is another layer of understanding and commitment to biblical living."

Howard Eyrich, DMin
Pastor of Counseling Ministries
www.howardeyrich.com

"My good friend Mark Shaw provides a rich, in-depth, and very practical workbook to help people who find themselves enslaved to their sin again after living in obedience and victory. The format of this workbook fosters meaningful interaction with the content for use in the counseling room, adult Sunday school curriculum, or small group settings. Mark is becoming a leading expert on nouthetically addressing addictions. This volume richly supplements his other outstanding books."

Rick Thomas, Founder and Executive Director,
Mt. Carmel Ministries, Grandview, MO

"Dr. Mark Shaw's goal is biblical transformation, not behavior modification. He exposes the heart attitudes that drive the habitual, destructive manner in which an addict satisfies instinctive, fleshly desires as the root of the problem, which is a worship disorder. He then shows how the sufficiency of Christ and Scriptures are to be understood in a very practical way. As a former addict/enslaved person myself, this book brought biblical conviction and understanding to my heart because of its scriptural truths. The title '*Relapse*' is appropriate because so many addicts are as 'dogs returning to vomit'. Mark helps to expose the beauty of Christ and worshiping Him over the inferior worship of idols. It is a very good, practical book and I highly recommend it."

Fred Bucci
Bachelor of Practical Ministry in Biblical Counseling, Master's Divinity School
Certified Biblical Counselor with NANC and IABC
Co-Founder, Elder and Counselor, Cornerstone Community Church,
Mayfield Heights, Ohio, Business Owner/Operator, 30 years, Cleveland, Ohio

Dedication

I want to dedicate this book first to my Lord and Savior Jesus Christ! He alone is awesome!

I cannot say "thank you" enough to my family: Mary and our four wonderful children; Ronny and Sandra Shaw, my giving parents; Matilda Mains, my loving grandmother; and Marie Eubank Turner, my gifted great Aunt. All of them are encouragers and so important to me!

Next, I want to thank my faith family: Shirley Crowder, Stan and Jan Haley, Shelley Berry, and the Truth in Love Ministries Board of Directors: Michael Fargarson, Jim Lowrey, Don Olvey, Jack Schreiner, and Rick Trotter. I am grateful also for the steady, loving leadership of Murray Smith and his wonderful bride, Nancy.

Also, I want to praise God for my mentors: Dr. Howard Eyrich, Dr. Harry Reeder, Lou Priolo, Ken Libby, and Don Bowen. God has blessed me to have learned from such godly men who walk with Christ.

Last but not least, I am grateful that God has crossed my path with Don Akenbrandt, Donn Arms, Michael Belzman, Gary Benedict, Bart Box, Fred Bucci, Richard Bunch, Chris Burns, Ben Deloach, Dan and Rosemary Gavin, Fred King, David Nasser, Chris Nichols, Martha Peace, David Platt, Robert Record, Jeff Robinson, Stuart Scott, Frank Smith, Brenda Lovelady Spahn, Keith Stanley, Randy Stinson, Deric Thomas, Rick Thomas (in MO), and Jay Younts. These people understand the importance of the Gospel in addiction counseling. Thank you, Lord, for these dedicated servants of Christ!

Foreword

Mark Shaw's latest workbook on Relapse is a breath of fresh air in a field that suffers from a deficit of clarity and truth in its literature. Our profession is wrought with differences of opinion that conflict with one another and deny the power Christ. In distinction to the panacea of false hope offered so often as therapeutic, his work penetrates to the heart of the matter in such a way that anyone who reads it seeking for authentic answers will find them. As an academic dean of a college focusing upon the specialized fields of Addiction and Biblical studies, I was satisfied that our curriculum was complete with the best textbooks available. But I have found through the books Mark has authored a voice of plain truth and insight that all people whose lives have been marked by addiction and deception most need to hear.

In a world that offers a myriad of false directions and confusions, Mark Shaw penetrates to the heart of the matter with wisdom and plain truth too often overlooked. **Relapse** is a must read, not only for people dealing with addiction in their own lives, but for those who hope to help them. Thank you, Mark, for what you have done for the ones who most need it. It is a true God-send to our profession.

In His Matchless Grace,
Rev. Michael Belzman, Ph.D., MDAAC, M-RAS
Founder / President
Association of Christian Alcohol & Drug Counselors Institute

Table of Contents

Introduction

There is much confusion today about "addiction." While most people think of it as a disease it is really an idea that is man-made and is less than 80 years old! The Christian must turn to the trusted Word of God that has been proven to be reliable and powerful over thousands of years and will never pass away!

Here are some words of instruction and caution as you read this book:

1) You must possess and understand three foundational principles in order to experience the transforming power and hope that is offered by Christ.

   a) You must be a committed follower of Christ to understand God's perspective on addiction and to gain insights that will bring lasting change into your life. If you are not a Christian, do not quit reading this book! Keep reading and read Appendix A daily until the Lord leads you to pray to confess and repent of your sins.

   b) You must believe in the supremacy of Scripture, the Holy Bible. This is God's Word, not mankind's words or best ideas! (Colossians 2:8)

   c) You must believe that it is through the partnership of the Holy Spirit, the Holy Scriptures, and your obedience to them that lasting change is made available to you. This is called sanctification (or growing in Christ) and it is a lifelong process.

2) You must be willing to dispense with the world's definitions of your problems and embrace what God says about your life. Using the non-biblical terms "substance abuser" and "addict" and "alcoholic" suggests that one is less responsible before God, and that is not true. The substance abuser and addict are responsible before God for the thoughts, words, and behaviors that led to becoming physically addicted to alcohol and drugs. Christians are capable of being *physically* addicted to a drug; therefore, the words "substance abuser" and "addict" will be utilized in this book with caution and with the understanding that God's answers for addiction are spiritual, powerful, practical, and hopeful for believers. Be conformed to God's ways and transformed by the renewing of your mind. Do not attempt to make God's ways conform to your desires. God is your sovereign, infinitely wise Creator.

3) Do not read this book without prayer support. Is there someone in your life right now (a trusted Christian friend, pastor, family member or loved one) who can commit to praying for you while you read and work through the concepts and instructions in this book? It may even be the person who gave you this book. Tell that person that you are reading this book and ask them to commit to praying for you daily until you finish it. This may be a year-long commitment (or more) so choose this person wisely.

4) It is not recommended that you read this book alone. Is there someone in your life right now (a Christian friend, pastor, family member or loved one) who can commit to walking with you through this period of time in your life as you seek God's answers for the addictive choices you have made? This may or may not be the same person described in #3 above. You might even need more than one person to fulfill this responsibility for the commitment. This

person needs to be a strong Christian person, have a deep love for God, and be willing to walk with you through this struggle. Prayerfully find this person before you go any further. You cannot isolate. You cannot do this alone. You need God and His mighty resources. Because the information in this book may be new and unfamiliar to you, you may need someone like a church leader or biblical counselor who will be able to answer spiritual questions that arise as you complete this study.

5) You must have a Bible on hand as you complete this relapse prevention workbook. I recommend that you purchase my other books to assist you in better understanding the biblical concepts presented in this book: *The Heart of Addiction*, *Cross Talking*, *Divine Intervention*, and *Addiction-Proof Parenting* are books that will help you. If you struggle with specific problems like cutting/self-injury, internet, TV, and videogame "addiction," and gambling, then I have specific booklets on those topics available to you as well in a *Hope and Help* series available through Focus Publishing (www.focuspublishing.com or 1-800-91-FOCUS). It may be helpful for you to purchase a separate prayer notebook and pen to journal your thoughts and feelings as you complete this workbook.

6) Your primary goal for changing your ways must be to please God and glorify Him in all your thoughts, words, and behaviors—not just to sober up and get your circumstances fixed. If your circumstances at this time have driven you to look for help, then know that our journey together will ultimately bring you to the place where all there is to life is fearing God and honoring Him by keeping His commandments. If this is not where you want to go, you need not read any further.

7) You must be planted and active in an evangelical, Bible teaching church, then ask your pastor for help (or ask him for help in finding someone who can help you) as you work through the concepts in this book. If you are not then begin to actively search for a Bible-teaching evangelical church. Once again, you cannot isolate during this transformation process. Jesus had disciples and He commanded His followers to make disciples and to teach others.[1] You and I need teachers in life. And you have a purpose and a place in the Body of Christ. We need you to be active and working in the Body of Believers called the Church! God made you to be relational and connected to others.

Use these 7 principles to sit down with a mentor and devise a customized "program" to follow to overcome addiction and prevent a relapse.

The purpose of this workbook is to help you understand the nature of what the world commonly calls relapse. The word "relapse" is only used in one Bible translation (NRSV), and then only twice![2] But Scripture is not otherwise silent on the concept of "relapse" because in essence it is a return to sin. Second Peter 2:22 illustrates, **"What the true proverb says has happened to them: 'The dog returns to its own vomit, and the sow, after washing herself, returns to wallow in the mire.'"** We are addressing relapse in the context of returning to a sin that has been repeated so often that the world lightly calls it an "addiction." The Bible deals with "addiction" as a sin originating in the heart. Drunkenness, idolatry, and sin are words the Lord uses to describe what the world only recently began calling "addiction."

---

[1] Matthew 28:19-20.

[2] Only *The New Revised Standard Version* of the Bible uses the English word "relapse" (occurring two times). Both instances, Judges 2:19 and 8:33, refer to the Israelites "relapsing" by returning to their sin of idolatrous worship of false gods and the sin of prostitution. "Relapse" in these two instances indicates a worsening by returning to sin!

Ultimately, the goal of this workbook is to help you to know God better. If you have relapsed recently, do not allow the enemy and the lies of this world to keep you down. Allow God to redeem you and restore you to fellowship with Him and others who love you. Consider your relapse to be one step backward, but then take two steps forward. Be like a boxer who gets back up after being knocked down.

If you have not relapsed, complete this workbook thinking about the last time you relapsed or sinned. Think of a specific time when you failed God and others by making a willful choice that was sinful. Refer back to the specific time that likely led to heartache for you as you answer the questions in this workbook.

Dr. Mark Shaw

Chapter One
What is Relapse?

Read any of the world's answers to relapse prevention and you will quickly find that "relapse" is a scary thing, a thing to be feared … a thing that will likely overtake you sooner or later unless you sign up for a program and go to certain meetings. The motivation to be clean and sober is fear-based—you must fear a relapse. But does fear ever motivate a person in a lasting way?

In Christianity, the motivation to be clean and sober is faith-based, out of love for God first and others second. In other words, your relationship with God must be your primary source of power and motivation for making better choices and right decisions that will honor Him. You must learn to walk by faith in Him. But how do you learn to trust Him?

Consider this: would you leave your wallet or purse with a complete stranger? The answer for most people is "No, of course not." Why? Because they contain valuable belongings that you would not want to lose; therefore, if a total stranger were to offer to watch your wallet or purse for you, you would probably say, "No, I can't do that because I don't know you." In a life of sobriety, the addicted person is required to trust God, but most addicts will not trust God with their wallets or purses, much less their lives!

If you think about it, this makes sense. Why would I trust God with my wallet or purse, much less my life, when I do not know God? That is asking a lot of someone who really only trusts himself. Why would anyone surrender their will to God's will and submit their lives to Him if they do not know Him? As a biblical counselor, I ask people to surrender to God, but they do not know Him and are not going to automatically trust Him.

Knowing God is crucial for being drug and alcohol free. If you have relapsed, then I know that you have failed to trust God. Instead, you chose to trust yourself. Maybe you have experienced so much harm and heartache at the abusive hands of others that you no longer believe you can trust anyone. That is precisely what the enemy would have you believe because that will isolate you and keep you from trusting God. More will be said about who you can trust as you read further in this workbook. (Proverbs 3:5-8)

The goal of this relapse prevention workbook is to help you to better know God so that you can better trust Him. Most importantly, He wants to reveal Himself to you through His Word of truth (the Bible) and the Holy Spirit. You must have those two ingredients—the Bible and the Holy Spirit—to better know who God is.

"Make me to know your ways, O LORD; teach me your paths" (Psalm 25:4).

Most secular relapse prevention programs emphasize knowledge in temporal[3] things. They emphasize knowledge of <u>warning signs</u>, "<u>triggers</u>," and <u>relapse prevention strategies</u>. All of that knowledge is good but only for

---

[3] Temporal is a biblical word meaning "temporary" or "related to life on this earth only." It will be used throughout this workbook.

a little while. The emphasis in this book is on the eternal knowledge you need first and foremost—knowledge of the Lord Jesus Christ! You need to put that knowledge into action! Just reading about something is not the same as doing something with that knowledge. Acting upon the knowledge of Christ is called walking by faith.

Do you know God? Can you trust Him? Knowledge of His character is a great starting point, but let me emphasize this: knowledge of Him *by itself* is insufficient. You must do something with that knowledge by putting it into practice by living in obedience to Him in your thinking, speaking, and doing. This is called living by faith and there is no substitute for faith in God. Hebrews 11:6 reminds you: **"And without faith it is impossible to please him, for whoever would draw near to God must believe that he exists and that he rewards those who seek him."** The people of the Bible who had faith in God trusted Him, obeyed Him, and made choices that looked foolish to the world but were right decisions in God's eyes (see Noah building an ark and Abraham leaving his homeland as two examples). You may have to look foolish in the world's eyes by making some radical choices, by faith, to obey Him, but He will be well-pleased when you do. Second Corinthians 5:9 states: **"So whether we are at home or away, we make it our aim to please him."** Your goal is to please God, and to glorify Him with your life.

Summary:
Your goal is to _____ God and glorify Him with your _____.

A relapse never happens by accident nor does it happen without displeasing God. It often hurts others, too, since a relapse rarely occurs in isolation. You are a relational being. You were created to have a relationship with God and with other people. If you relapsed recently, then it is likely you made choices that were centered upon pleasing yourself rather than pleasing God or others. God is ready to forgive you through the shed blood of the Lord Jesus Christ and ready to empower you through the Holy Spirit working in partnership with the Word of God. This workbook is simply a tool to re-direct you back to trusting in Almighty God, who is your loving heavenly Father.

You were created to have a _____with God and with other _____.

Relapse Defined

For one to relapse, a person has to have first attained sobriety for a period of time. Someone who never achieved a sober period of time and continues to use and abuse drugs or any type of "addictive" pleasure is not relapsing. They are still in active addiction. However, one who has achieved a significant period of sobriety and returns back to the addictive pleasure has relapsed.

A biblical proverb aptly describes relapse in this manner: **"The dog returns to its own vomit, and the sow, after washing herself, returns to wallow in the mire"** (2 Peter 2:22b). After experiencing the freedom of a sober lifestyle, a person who relapses is choosing to return to the voluntary slavery of addiction. The word "relapse" is defined as "the act or an instance of backsliding, worsening, or subsiding."[4]

---

[4] Merriam-Webster, I. (1996, c1993). *Merriam-Webster's Collegiate Dictionary.* Includes index (10th ed.). Springfield, Mass., U.S.A.: Merriam-Webster.

Personally, I do not like the term "relapse" because it has a secondary meaning that misleads most people into thinking that it is purely a physical problem when in reality it is a spiritual problem of the soul. This second definition of "relapse" is defined as "a recurrence of symptoms of a disease after a period of improvement."[5] The word "relapse" has the medical implication that addiction is a disease with symptoms. A medical doctor once said that physicians do a great job addressing problems in the physical body but they should never try to address addiction issues and emotional issues because those are matters of the soul. In other words, they are spiritual issues, not physical issues, and I believe he is right! No pill in the world empowers a person to make right choices because addiction is not merely a physical problem altered by medicine but a spiritual problem in the heart, or inner person. In fact, every individual is solely responsible to God to make right choices!

Some people think a relapse is a physical problem when it is really a _____ problem.

Ultimately, we all are going to answer to God in the next life for what we choose to do in this one. The little choices we make have big, eternal consequences. In Luke 16:1-13, Jesus taught a parable that concluded with: **"One who is faithful in a very little is also faithful in much, and one who is dishonest in a very little is also dishonest in much."** Jesus was talking about the stewardship of money in terms of how temporal decisions in this life indicate whether a person will be faithful with eternal riches. The choices a person makes with temporary wealth will reveal the priorities in his heart regarding eternal things. Jesus went further to say in verse 13, **"No servant can serve two masters, for either he will hate the one and love the other, or he will be devoted to the one and despise the other. You cannot serve God and money."**

Likewise, in a relapse, the choice a person makes to satisfy a temporal pleasure reveals a momentary loss of eternal perspective. All relapses involve a decision to live for the moment without regard for the far-reaching consequences and damage in this life and in the life to come. The reputation of God is damaged when a Christian makes a temporal choice deciding to relapse. This type of choice is akin to Esau in Genesis 25:29-34: **"Once when Jacob was cooking stew, Esau came in from the field, and he was exhausted. And Esau said to Jacob, 'Let me eat some of that red stew, for I am exhausted!' (Therefore his name was called Edom.) Jacob said, 'Sell me your birthright now.' Esau said, 'I am about to die; of what use is a birthright to me?' Jacob said, 'Swear to me now.' So he swore to him and sold his birthright to Jacob. Then Jacob gave Esau bread and lentil stew, and he ate and drank and rose and went his way. Thus Esau despised his birthright."**

Your choice to satisfy a temporal pleasure reveals a momentary loss of _____ _____.

In this biblical passage, Esau's words to his brother to trade his birthright, or future inheritance, for a measly bowl of soup to meet a temporal hunger

---

[5]Ibid.

pain demonstrated Esau's attitude toward eternal things. A birthright not only represented the wealth Esau would have in this life but the eternal blessing available to him in the next life. Yet Esau did not care about anything other than meeting a temporary desire for food. People who relapse are making the same decision. They are choosing a temporal pleasure over the promises of God. In other words, they are refusing to walk by faith and choosing to walk by sight: "Give me that pleasure now and I'll risk eternity and the consequences I'll have to face later."

A relapse is a choice to satisfy a temporary _____ that you have already declared to be _____ to your well-being.

When you consider that the Word of God declares a "relapse" to be sin, then you see that it is a choice to satisfy a temporary desire that you have already declared to be dangerous to your own well-being, the well-being of others, and damaging to the reputation of God. That relapse may be motivated by the desire to avoid pain or to seek pleasure, but, in either case, it is often sinful.[6] Drunkenness, sexual immorality, and gluttony are sins. They are acts of the will for which every person is accountable to God.

The Word of God calls sin a willful choice to disobey and not trust God. Disobeying God is always rooted in doubting God and not trusting Him. Many who sin think that they will get away with it. They are willing to risk the consequences just to achieve a temporary pleasure, or high. What about you? Why did you relapse?

"Desire without knowledge is not good, and whoever makes haste with his feet, misses his way" (Proverbs 19:2).

In the space provided, write out the details of the situation you were in when you first chose to willfully "relapse:" where you were, who you were with, what you were doing, why you were there, etc. Give as many details as possible except when your details may involve or hurt others:

What were you thinking prior to your choice to relapse?

What were you feeling (emotions) prior to your relapse?

What were some of your actions that made it easier for you to relapse prior to the actual event?

---

[6] Note that not all temporary pleasures (like the use of a drug, sex within marriage, or eating a dessert) are sinful. God looks at the heart of mankind (1 Samuel 16:7) and knows if it is sinful or not. Of course, blatant drunkenness, sexual immorality, and gluttony are always sinful. For more clarification on the good purpose of drugs and alcohol, read chapter 6 of *The Heart of Addiction*.

What were some of the words you said (whether out loud to someone else, or in your heart to yourself) prior to your relapse?

Finally, and most importantly, what did you want to achieve, gain, or experience prior to your relapse? In other words, examine your will and the strong desires in your heart. What were they?

Do you still have this heart's desire?

One final note: a relapse does NOT have to mean utter defeat. Getting knocked down in a boxing match is not defeat. We are defeated when we do not try to get up and get back in the fight. Quitting is not an option in this life! Even in relapse the Lord has a redemptive plan for you, meaning that He wants to bring good from the bad choice(s) you made. Only God can take our sins and save our lives in spite of them. He wants to do that for you now.

> Even in relapse, God has a _____ plan for you.

In Genesis 37:12-36, Joseph's own brothers sold him into slavery. They sinned against Joseph and against God. Their sin was shameful, as they sold their brother for money and he then became a slave in a foreign land. They lied about it to their father, who loved Joseph and who was heartbroken to hear that his son was gone. They hid their sin for years from their family. However, when they were reunited with Joseph years later, he reminded them that what they had meant for evil, God had meant for good: **"As for you, you meant evil against me, but God meant it for good, to bring it about that many people should be kept alive, as they are today"** (Genesis 50:20). In fact, their evil act actually saved their lives! Had they not sinned against Joseph, they would have likely died in a famine. God not only used their sin to save them but He used the forgiveness of Joseph to demonstrate His love and forgiveness to them. Only God redeems our bad choices and brings good out of them. He will do the same for you as you address your heart's desires and learn to surrender them to God by seeking forgiveness from Him on a moment by moment basis.

Forgiveness

Think about your most recent relapse episode as you answer the questions below:

> God used the forgiveness of Joseph to demonstrate His _____ and _____ to the brothers.

1. What part of your thinking, words, and actions were sinful according to the Bible?

2. Have you asked God to forgive you based upon the blood sacrifice of the Lord Jesus Christ? _____. If not, pray now and ask Him to forgive your thoughts, words, and actions and be specific!

3. Read 1 John 1:8. What two things does this verse say about us if we deny that we have sin in us?

   A.

   B.

4. Read 1 John 1:9. What two things does this verse say God will do for you when you confess your sin?

   A.

   B.

5. Read Proverbs 28:13. This verse says that someone who conceals their sin will NOT prosper. What two actions does this verse recommend a person take to find mercy?

   A.

   B.

6. Proverbs 28:13 tells you to confess with your words (mouth) and to forsake (or repent) with your actions. When you speak a confession and then "do" the confession through your actions, you are considered to be repentant and you will find mercy. Words alone without the actions will not suffice. You must be a doer of the Word and not just a hearer only. Write out James 1:22 in the space provided and memorize it:

7. Write down the definition of the word "advocate" from a dictionary in the space provided:

8. Write down 1 John 2:1 in the space provided:

9. Now, look up the word "mediator" in the dictionary and write its definition in the space provided:

10. Write out 1 Timothy 2:5 in the space provided below:

"But each person is tempted when he is lured and enticed by his own desire. Then desire when it has conceived gives birth to sin, and sin when it is fully grown brings forth death" (James 1:14-15).

For more on the topic of addiction as a sin, please refer to the following books by the author available through Focus Publishing:

The Heart of Addiction: A Biblical Perspective
Cross Talking: A Daily Gospel for Transforming Addicts
Addiction-Proof Parenting: Biblical Prevention Strategies
Divine Intervention: Hope and Help for Families of Addicts
Hope and Help for Self-Injurers and "Cutters"

Also helpful is the book, *A Banquet in the Grave,* by Edward Welch.

Chapter Two
The Importance of Christian Fellowship

A discipleship relationship is vitally important for you to rebound from a relapse and prevent it from occurring again in the future. In this chapter we will learn how important it is to have a close relationship with a fellow Christian who will help and encourage you as you grow in strength and knowledge of God's will for your life.

We have already established that when we use the word "addiction" we are referring to not just the medical, physical problems associated with addictive choices, but primarily a spiritual problem. While it does have physical elements, an addiction is really a choice of your will to obey the flesh and deny the commands of the Holy Spirit. Addiction is a "choice problem" in your will that causes you to be enslaved physically and emotionally to the idolatrous pleasure. For Christians, there is a war waging between their old nature characterized by the "flesh," and their new nature, characterized by the indwelling Holy Spirit. Galatians 5:16-17 puts it this way: **"But I say, walk by the Spirit, and you will not gratify the desires of the flesh. For the desires of the flesh are against the Spirit, and the desires of the Spirit are against the flesh, for these are opposed to each other, to keep you from doing the things you want to do."**

Some people mistakenly think that once you become a Christian sin is no longer a problem, but the opposite is actually true. The enemy of your soul will not be content to leave you alone. The difference between a Christian who sins and an unbeliever who sins is that the Christian feels badly about his sinful choices. This "bad" feeling, as many often call it, is actually a good thing called "conviction" and it is from the Holy Spirit. This conviction is meant to bring about a change commonly called repentance. God wants to bring us to our knees in repentance, prayer, Bible reading, and obedience to Him because He knows that conviction will ultimately bring Him glory and transform us into His image. Consider just one aspect of the Holy Spirit's role in the lives of men according John 16:7-9: **"Nevertheless, I tell you the truth: it is to your advantage that I go away, for if I do not go away, the Helper will not come to you. But if I go, I will send him to you. And when he comes, he will convict the world concerning sin and righteousness and judgment: concerning sin, because they do not believe in me."** Jesus is telling His disciples that He must go away but that He will send the Helper, the Holy Spirit, to come, and the Holy Spirit will bring conviction of sin. That is simply one function of the Holy Spirit in our lives: to bring conviction of sin.

This conviction is a good thing. If you are driving down a road and the bridge is out, wouldn't you want someone to warn you? If you were unaware of it and kept driving, you could die. God warns us by His Holy Spirit's conviction of sinful choices we are considering or have already

Circle one:
Addiction is a
a) Choice problem
b) Sin problem
c) Both

The "bad" feeling you get when you sin is really _____ of the Holy Spirit.

"Sin is blatant mutiny against God." Oswald Chambers

made. God wants us to repent, or to change our thinking which will lead to a change in actions. He knows that is the best way for us to live since sin brings separation from God and others.

In Genesis 3, sin is accurately depicted for us in the historical account of Adam and Eve. Before their sinful choices, Adam and Eve lived in perfect unity with each other and harmony with God. They walked with God in the garden in the cool of the day. They had intimate knowledge of and fellowship with each other and God. But something happened. They were tempted to doubt the Word of God and they chose to disobey Him. They were taking a risk when they took matters into their own hands. They wanted to do what they wanted to do in their own will rather than obey God's will. The result was separation from each other through the covering of fig leaves and separation from God through hiding, according to Genesis 3:7-8: **"Then the eyes of both were opened, and they knew that they were naked. And they sewed fig leaves together and made themselves loincloths. And they heard the sound of the LORD God walking in the garden in the cool of the day, and the man and his wife hid themselves from the presence of the LORD God among the trees of the garden."**

This break of intimate fellowship only occurred after their sinful choices were made. God had not changed, yet Adam and Eve had changed as a result of sin. They no longer trusted each other or trusted God. It was evident that they trusted themselves more than they trusted God; otherwise, they would not have chosen to disobey Him. Sin only happens when we think we know better than God and we decide to trust ourselves. Sin is always a decision to trust our self more than God and it is never an accident. That is why God holds us responsible for our sinful choices no matter what the circumstances may be.

In life's circumstances you are always choosing how to respond to: 1) your own sinful choices and the consequences, and 2) how the sinful choices of others which impact you. In other words, when we are experiencing problems, we are either sinning ourselves or being sinned against by someone else, or both! We need to know how to deal with each of these, especially when learning to prevent relapse since we are relational beings.

Exercise:

Analyze your recent past by thinking of a specific problem or relapse situation that has occurred in the past weeks or days. What problems have occurred as a result of this situation? Describe them in the space provided:

Were any of those problems caused by your own sin? _____

After Adam and Eve sinned they lost intimate _____ with God.

Sin is always a decision to trust _____ more than God. God holds us responsible for our sinful _____.

"When the sense of guilt drives a man to God, to duty, to the throne of grace, then the darkness will not be long with that man."
Thomas Brooks, 1665

Were any of those problems caused as a result of someone else's sinful choices against you? _____

In either case, reflect upon how you responded relationally to others. Did you separate or pull away from God as a result of these problematic situations? What were your "fig leaves" that you used to conceal your sin (Proverbs 28:13)?

Did you separate or pull away from another person as a result of these problematic situations?

Since sin always brings separation. Did you experience loneliness either after you sinned or were sinned against? _____ What did you do in response to your loneliness?

I strongly suggest that you not try to prevent relapse alone. Loneliness is a place where we are vulnerable to the temptations of the enemy and prone to make poor and sinful choices. God made us to be in relationship with Him and with others. We were not created to live on an island all by ourselves and, when we do, we are prone to trust and depend only upon ourselves and not upon God or other people. Satan loves to isolate us and separate us because he knows we are weak when we are alone. Sheep tend to stay together and, like sheep, we in the body of Christ must stay close together. We must learn to live in intimate fellowship in peaceful relationships with each other. When we sin or someone sins against us, we must speak the truth in love.

Our goal should be to prevent relapse without the help of others.
Circle One
    True   False

If your sin has caused your loneliness, pray and ask God to speak to you through His Word and Spirit. John 4:23-24 states: **"But the hour is coming, and is now here, when the true worshipers will worship the Father in spirit and truth, for the Father is seeking such people to worship him. God is spirit and those who worship him must worship in spirit and truth."** Those who return to right fellowship with God do so through worshiping Him in spirit and in truth.

"But if we walk in the light, as he is in the light, we have fellowship with one another, and the blood of Jesus his Son cleanses us from all sin" (1 John 1:7).

It is important to find a trusted Christian friend (TCF) or good biblical counselor who is able to **"speak the truth in love"** to you so that you relationally learn the truth that is in Christ Jesus in order to grow spiritually (Ephesians 4:11-21). We grow spiritually by reading and studying His Word. God created us to have vibrant, learning relationships with others, and not to live in isolation. God wants you to be a student who is discipled by a more mature Christian so that you can learn who Christ is, what He requires of

His followers, and how you can implement His Word in a practical manner in your life. God did not create us to cope with life's trials on our own, which is why He provided access to Him through the Holy Spirit and the family of faith which is a local church of Christians.

Being "confrontable" means you are able to receive _____ given in _____.

A good TCF or biblical counselor will share with you the truth of God's Word saturated in the love of the Holy Spirit so that you look to Christ to find the answers to your problems. If the truth of God's Word is not presented in the love of the Holy Spirit, then your TCF or biblical counselor has failed to accurately show you who Christ is. It is not the truth *and* love, as though they are separate, but the truth *in* love that you need to experience, and your biblical counselor relies upon the Holy Spirit and God's Word for both. You must be receptive and teachable in this relationship and not allow yourself to be too sensitive while you are growing in Christ. You may need to be confronted with the truth in love in order to bring lasting change, so

Overly sensitive people are often _____ which hinders _____ growth.

you must be "confrontable,"[7] meaning that you must be able to receive the feedback given in love. Overly sensitive people are often prideful, which impedes spiritual growth. Learning humility is an essential element of a life transformed from addiction.

Are you involved in a local church? _____

Do you have a person who is discipling you (teaching you in close relationship) how to live out the Word of God? _____

If not, list 3 people of your same gender that you consider to be spiritually mature believers:

1) _____
2) _____
3) _____

Contact each person one at a time and ask them to disciple you. You do not have to say, "I'm an addict and need a sponsor." Instead, ask them, "I am a new believer and I need to be taught the Word of God and how to live it. Will you disciple me in the Bible?"

It may take more than three people so keep asking other people in your church until you find someone who will agree to disciple you. (Very important note: pick someone to disciple you who is your same gender. Men need other men to disciple them and women need other women.)

---

[7] "Confrontable" is not a real word but is my word to describe how someone must be open and willing to receive constructive criticism, feedback, or the truth spoken in love from someone who is discipling them to follow Christ.

Once you have established fellowship, this trusted Christian friend (TCF) is someone who is going to teach you to follow Jesus so that you can become like Jesus in how you think, speak, and act. Your obligation to the person who is discipling you is to do what they say to do. You must submit your will to God, and a practical way to do this is by submitting your will to this person. As long as your TCF does not tell you to sin, you need to do what he or she is asking of you.

For more on submission, read Chapter 20 in *The Heart of Addiction* and Day 33 in *Cross Talking*.

Submission is not forced. Submission is a choice. For example, when a driver comes to a yield sign, he has a choice. He must slow down and look to see if any other cars are coming. His will is to keep moving but he recognizes that he must stop, think, and look prior to driving ahead. Likewise, you must yield your will to God, and you do this in a practical way through yielding to the person the Lord has sent to disciple you. If your disciple-maker tells you to do something that is not a sin, you need to do it even if you do not like it.

The root word in "discipleship" is common to the word for "discipline." If you relapsed recently, then one thing is clear: you lack discipline in your life. This disciple-maker is God's provision for you to learn to be more disciplined. It will take this type of committed relationship for you to grow spiritually in order to prevent relapse.

If you have relapsed recently, one thing is clear: you lack _____ in your life.

Why must you do what this person asks? Imagine you are teaching someone to play the piano. You give a piano lesson and tell your student, "I will see you next week. In the meantime, practice what you have learned today." The student returns the next week but did not practice at all to build the basic skills necessary to become a good pianist. As a teacher, what can you do? You cannot build upon the previous lesson because nothing was practiced. Likewise, as someone who needs to be discipled, you must practice what you have been taught or else the relationship will be fruitless and frustrating to the disciple-maker and to you.

List your expectations and goals for this relationship with your disciple-maker:

Ask your disciple-maker to list his/her expectations and goals for this relationship:

Now, be specific and ask your disciple-maker to help you make a list of areas to address in the next 6 weeks. What areas of your life need to be addressed? Where will you begin?

Examples:
- I need to learn to make decisions without allowing my emotions to rule me.
- I need to learn to submit. I need to stop blaming others.
- I need to be more thankful in my words and thoughts.

Write out at least 5 areas to change in your life in the space provided.

Now list specific objectives and measurable goals to grow in each of these areas:

Examples:
- I will make a list of people and things for which I am thankful (Philippians 4:8).
- I will read a chapter of Proverbs every day.
- I will meet with my TCF for discipleship once per week.

Chapter Three
Transformation vs. Recovery

The goal of this workbook is to help you to grow in new relationships and build new habits of thinking, speaking, and acting so that you never go back to addictive behavior. In order to do this, you must understand biblical words and concepts and reject the ideas of the world. Words have meaning and when Scripture says **"the Word became flesh"** it identifies Jesus as the physical manifestation of the Word of God. In fact, words are so important that God used His words to create the world in which we live (Genesis 1:3, 6, 9, 11, 14, 20, 24, 26, 28, and 29). Jesus did not live in an era of cameras and pictures, wants us to value His Word, not pictures or symbols of Him! His Words are to live within us as He Himself is living within us. According to John 15:7: **"If you abide in me, and my words abide in you, ask whatever you wish, and it will be done for you."**

One of the most profound mysteries in all of science is the way a caterpillar is transformed into a butterfly. This once and for all process, metamorphosis, can be likened to the transformation that occurred in the life of the Apostle Paul, who was transformed like few others in history. He was a man who formerly killed Christians but was radically transformed by the Person and Power of Jesus Christ to become one of the greatest proponents of Christianity. In that instance, God renamed Paul, who used to be called Saul (Acts 13:9). Like Paul, God gives us a new identity through the righteousness of Christ.

Romans 12:2 states: **"Do not be conformed to this world, but be <u>transformed</u> by the renewal of your mind, that by testing you may discern what is the will of God, what is good and acceptable and perfect."** One of the central messages of Christianity is that God wants us to "be transformed" into a new creation in Christ Jesus. Second Corinthians 5:17 states: **"Therefore, if anyone is in Christ, he is a new creation. The old has passed away; behold, the new has come."** Note that this transformation is both an immediate occurrence at salvation (2 Corinthians 5:17) *and* an ongoing process of growing in Christ after salvation (Romans 12:2). Because of habitual sin, you must be transformed daily by the power of the Holy Spirit who renews your mind.

The command in Scripture to be transformed applies to all people struggling with "addiction" problems. My primary goal in writing this relapse prevention workbook, the daily devotional, and other books on the topic of "addiction," is to show you that the Lord wants you to be transformed from being an "addict" (and it applies to being addicted to anything really) into being like His Son. In other words, your identity is in Christ if you are a Christian, and your purpose is found only in the Word of Christ.

"Contemporary Christians have been caught in the spurious logic that those who have found Him need no longer seek Him."
A.W. Tozer

The goal of this workbook is to help you grow in new _____and build new _____ of thinking, _____ and _____ so that you never go back to addictive behavior.

God does not want you to be _____ to this world, but instead, to be _____ by the renewal of your _____ (Romans 12:2).

"Recovery" is the buzz word in secular addiction counseling. Recovery means "to regain or to recapture one's old self."[8] For physical healing, "recovery" is a good word, for it implies an improvement in your condition. For spiritual healing, however, we find a better word in the Word of God. Scripture teaches that God desires more for us than "recovery" or that we recapture our old self, because even when we "recover" our old self, we are left with just that—our old self. God desires a total transformation.

To transform something is to change its "character or condition."[9] Even the word "reform" is inadequate for what God desires to do in an addict's heart because to "reform" something is simply to "change into an improved form or condition."[10] Again, reform is a good word. But for the Christian, God wants more. God wants transformation. He wants you to experience His transforming power to make you more like Christ and an entirely new creation.

Our new life in Christ looks nothing like who we were in our flesh. Just improving the flesh is not God's best for you; He wants you to be completely different than you once were. It is a spiritual change brought about by the power of the Holy Spirit. Notice the word "transformed" in 2 Corinthians 3:18: **"And we all, with unveiled face, beholding the glory of the Lord, are being <u>transformed</u> into the same image from one degree of glory to another. For this comes from the Lord who is the Spirit."**

A "transformation" is God's answer for any and all types of "addiction." The "transformation" is a lifelong process that begins when you are no longer thinking like the world, but thinking about and viewing life correctly—as God thinks about and views it—as revealed in His Word of Truth, the Bible. I encourage you to pray as you read this book daily so that it will teach you what the Bible says regarding God's perspective for overcoming your "addiction." My prayer for you is that you will allow God's Word to renew the thinking in your mind, experience the love of the Holy Spirit as you read, and then do what the Lord leads you to do daily, which will "transform" you into Christ-likeness so that He will be glorified through your life.

According to Romans 8:29a, God's desire for you is to become like Christ: **"For those whom he foreknew he also predestined to be conformed to the image of his Son."** Like a potter molds clay into the shape of a pot so will God mold you into the image of His Son throughout your lifetime as you grow spiritually (Romans 9:20-21). The Lord's goal for you is not simply to cope with relapse "triggers" and temptations for the remainder of your life, but to empower you by His Spirit to have sustaining power from Him to say "no" to your temptations to choose sin while saying "yes" to your new life in Christ.

"Recovery" means to regain or _____ one's old self.

To "transform" something means to "change its _____ or _____."

"Character is what you are in the dark." D.L. Moody

---

[8] Merriam-Webster, I. (1996, c1993). *Merriam-Webster's Collegiate Dictionary*. Includes index (10th ed.). Springfield, Mass., U.S.A.: Merriam-Webster.

[9] Ibid.

[10] Ibid.

Colossians 3:3 reminds all Christians that they lose their old identity and find a new identity in Christ: **"For you have died, and your life is hidden with Christ in God."** This transformation only happens as the struggling addict surrenders everything to Christ and adopts an eternal perspective rather than a temporal perspective that seeks pleasure or avoids pain. Colossians 3:1-2 says: **"If then you have been raised with Christ, seek the things that are above, where Christ is, seated at the right hand of God. Set your minds on things that are above, not on things that are on earth."** Be intentional in setting your thoughts (mind) upon eternity and not on the pleasures of this earth.

God wants you to find a new identity in _____ so you will have a perspective that is _____ and not _____.

What is eternal in your life?

In the room where you are right now, I guarantee there is at least one eternal "thing," and that is your soul. If anyone else is present with you, then that person's soul is eternal, too. God's Word and the Holy Spirit are eternal. Buildings, books, televisions, phones, and other objects are not eternal. Even your physical body is not eternal, since your soul will be given a new body that is imperishable in the next life (1 Corinthians 15:35-49).

In light of eternity, what decisions in your past would you change if you could, based upon what you know about their consequences now? List 3 to 5 below:

Do you know that although God forgives you for your sinful choices, you may still have to experience the consequences of those choices for the remainder of your life?

If you throw a rock into a body of water, ripples are produced that cannot be stopped. Likewise, you may wish that you could take back the "thrown rock" decisions you have made in your life since the "ripple" consequences are already in place. However, you need to view these decisions in your life in light of the redemptive power of God. In other words, only God has the power to make good out of the bad decisions you have made. Romans 8:28 speaks to the redemptive power of God in a Christian's life: **"And we know that for those who love God all things work together for good, for those who are called according to his purpose."** Be sure to note that this

"I will restore to you the years that the swarming locust has eaten…" *(Joel 2:25a).*

promise is ONLY for those who love God. The promise is not for those who do not love God.

Do you love God? _____

Can you see His redemptive power in your life despite some bad decisions you have made? List 3 to 5 examples below:

How does knowing that God redeems your bad choices encourage you?

"To do it no more is the truest repentance." Martin Luther

If you know that God redeems your bad choices, should you continue to sin?

Read Romans 6:1-2 and write these verses out in the space provided:

What does Romans 6:1-2 tell us about the grace of God regarding whether we should continue to sin or not?

List by priority the names of the people with eternal souls whom you want to share the Gospel message of forgiveness and transformation? List up to 10 persons below:

1) _____
2) _____
3) _____
4) _____
5) _____
6) _____
7) _____
8) _____
9) _____
10) _____

Christians are grateful for the mercy and grace of God. Mercy means that we do NOT receive what we deserve for our sins (i.e. Christians are not punished since Jesus experienced the wrath of God on the cross). His grace means that we DO receive what we do NOT deserve (i.e. Christians experience the goodness and favor of God in their lives). God's grace is given to undeserving sinners, even those who have relapsed! Romans 5:8 gives us another glimpse into the grace of God: **"but God shows his love for us in that while we were still sinners, Christ died for us."** In other words, we do not "get right" and then experience the grace of God, but rather, it is the opposite: we are wrong and receive the grace of God while we are yet sinners. So do not think you must get right from your relapse and then go to God. Go to Him now through a prayer of repentance, confessing your sins and asking Him to empower you to overcome your sin of addiction. Write out a prayer from your heart in the space provided and pray it now:

God's <u>mercy</u> means not getting the wrath we _____ for our sins.

God's <u>grace</u> means getting what we do not _____ for our sins.

Dear Father God,

Notes

Chapter Four
Identifying Your Enemy

Have you come to understand how lost and hopeless life is without the power of Christ Jesus? Have you tried everything in the world's textbooks for "addiction" and yet still failed miserably? In this chapter, you will learn how to battle your primary enemy. According to the Bible, we all have three enemies: Satan, the world's system, and our own flesh. The battle with addiction is not easy because you are fighting three enemies, not one. Guess which of these three enemies is your most difficult opponent:

_____

If you guessed Satan or the world in the space above, you would be wrong. It may surprise you that your most challenging enemy is your flesh. Most people do not view themselves as their own worst enemy. Instead, they view demons and outside influences as primary enemies when, in reality, you are your own worst enemy. You are the problem. Christ is the solution, and the power of the Holy Spirit working in your heart to change you is your only hope.

List the 3 enemies the Bible says we all have:

1)

2)

3)

Satan is a powerful enemy but, simply put, Satan has no spiritual authority over the Christian. People who say "the devil made me do it" do not understand their own sinful habits in the flesh and the power that these habits have inside of them. In James 4:7, the Word of God tells us to deal with Satan in the following manner: **"Submit yourselves therefore to God. Resist the devil, and he will flee from you."** In other words, your job is to submit and surrender to God. When you do His will and not your own, then the devil will be resisted and he will flee from you. Remember that Satan's tactics are not to overpower you spiritually but to make you doubt the very Word of God. Satan wants to plant a simple seed of doubt in your mind about God's will for your life. He might ask, "Can God really be trusted? Does God have your best interest in mind?" Satan would also encourage you to "trust in yourself" since you obviously have "your own best interests in mind" and "you think you know better than God what is best for you."

Recall that in Genesis 3:1, Satan tempted Eve who ate the apple and gave to Adam. He planted a seed of doubt about the goodness of God and appealed to her desire to do her own will. In Matthew 4:1-11, when Satan tempted Jesus, he challenged Jesus to do his own will and not the will of God the Father. The temptations for you are the same. Satan doesn't care whether you believe in him or not. He simply wants you to do your own will, not God's. Satan wants you to trust yourself, not God.

"Submit yourselves therefore to _____, resist the _____ and he will _____ from you" (James 4:7).

In Matthew 26:39, Jesus, as a man, was required to place his human will aside in order to do the will of God the Father, which was to go to the cross: **"And going a little farther he fell on his face and prayed, saying, 'My Father, if it be possible, let this cup pass from me; nevertheless,**

not as I will, but as you will.'" That statement by Jesus should astound you. In another translation it says, **"Not my will, but your will be done."** Jesus trusted the Father because He knew the Father is loving and good. Do you know the Father? Do you trust the Father? The Bible encourages you to trust the Father *more than you trust yourself* just as Jesus trusted the Father's will more than His own will as a man.

Another enemy we face is the world's system, or the belief system and lies of this world. If you are in love with the world and the temporal things it has to offer, you are committing spiritual adultery with the world's pleasures and being unfaithful to God. If you are a Christian, you are considered to be the bride of Christ. You are married to Christ.

"But your iniquities have made a separation between you and your God, and your sins have hidden his face from yu so that he does not hear"(Isaiah 59:2).

James 4:4 confirms this principle: **"You adulterous people! Do you not know that friendship with the world is enmity with God? Therefore whoever wishes to be a friend of the world makes himself an enemy of God."** When someone is adulterous, they are treating another person they are not married to as though that person is their spouse. That is what is going on when one entertains a friendship of sinning with the world's pleasures rather than obeying God who calls us to deny ourselves and to follow Him. To go with the folly of the world is putting yourself in opposition to God, and that makes you one of His enemies. Here is a news flash: God's enemies never win!

Since your flesh is your greatest enemy you must learn to love what God loves (_____) and hate what God hates (_____).

Then who is your primary enemy? The answer is your flesh, or your will to please your flesh. You must learn to say "no" to the desires of your flesh and say "yes" to the desires, leading, and love of the Holy Spirit who lives in you once you are saved. You must learn to say "not my will, but your will be done, Lord," just as Jesus said it. Your will lives in your "heart," biblically speaking. I am not referring to a physical, beating organ, but to your inner person that contains your desires, attitudes, thoughts, and feelings. This is where your will is. So you must learn to love what God loves (righteousness) and to hate what God hates (sin). You must value His reputation as more important than your own. You must adopt His will and not your own.

What are some examples of how your will has conflicted with God's will in your past, especially related to relapse, if applicable?

List some of the lies you have believed (or acted upon) in the past:

Your past can no longer define you. Your past is not who you are if you are a Christian. Christians find their identity in Christ alone, not in themselves or apart from Him. Do your spouse, children, job, or past sins define you? If so, you must make the choice to find your new identity in Christ.

After reading the following scriptures, write a quick statement about who God says that you are in Christ:

What do these same verses say about God and his character? List His attributes below:

John 1:12	
1 Corinthians 3:16	
1 Corinthians 6:17	
Galatians 2:20	
Ephesians 1:1	
Ephesians 1:5	
Philippians 1:6	
Colossians 1:14	
Colossians 3:3	
1 John 5:18	

The Battle Within

Where do you run to when your primary enemy is inside of you? The answer is to Christ and the cross. Run to Him! Run to Jesus Christ and lay your sins at the foot of the cross. One of the most encouraging teachings of the Bible is that the Lord puts His Spirit to dwell within us to empower us to overcome the sinful desires of our own will. Second Timothy 1:14 says: **"By the Holy Spirit who dwells within us, guard the good deposit entrusted to you."**

If you are a Christian, there is no longer a battle for your soul. There is a battle for your _____ _____.

This is where the real battle exists: inside of you. Your old habits in your flesh war against the new Spirit inside of you. There is no longer a battle for your soul if you are a Christian; instead, there is a battle for your spiritual growth. I often pray that I want less of me and more of Christ in my life. Really, we are to crucify, or put to death, our flesh (Galatians 5:24). So I want none of me and all of Christ ruling my heart and my will.

How do we
- Get to know God
- Become like Christ
- Learn to live obedient lives for God's glory?

By _____
the Word of _____.

The best way to feed your spirit rather than your flesh is through reading the Bible. The Bible gives you understanding of the mind, or very thoughts, of God. But you can only understand and discern the truth of the Bible by the power of the Holy Spirit. There are people who have memorized the Bible but do not understand truth simply because they do not have the Holy Spirit living inside of them. Reading the Bible is how you know God. The Bible is God's Word and it is written to help us to know Him, to change us to become like Christ, and learn to live obedient lives for the glory of God.

Here is how it works: God gave you a will. Out of your will flow strong desires that lead you to think about what you want. As you think about what you want, you devise a plan for accomplishing your will. Your thoughts lead to words and/or actions. Those words and actions lead to emotions. Ultimately, you are to respond to those feelings, or emotions, in a way that pleases God.[11] Let me give you two examples.

Let's look at Tommy. He wants to act on his strong desire for his addictive pleasure though he knows it is sinful and wrong. He thinks about how good it will feel and how he can escape from the problems in his life just for a little while. He devises a plan to carry out his will. His thoughts are consumed with accomplishing his will and he follows through with words and actions. Tommy gets his addictive pleasure and enjoys it for a little while. Then, when he comes out of that period of pleasure, his emotions rise to the surface. He realizes that he feels guilty, ashamed, fearful, depressed, and even a little bit angry. All of these emotions are a result of his sinful choice that began in his will. He is experiencing the conviction of the Holy Spirit (John 16:8).

"Blessed is the man who remains steadfast under trial, for when he has stood the test he will receive the crown of life, which God has promised to those who love him"(James 1:12).

Like Tommy in the example above, write out 1 or 2 personal examples of how your will led to thoughts, words, actions, and eventually to emotions.

Example of Tommy:

My Will	Addictive Pleasure
My Thoughts	I want to call my friend. I want to feel good again.
My Words	"Friend, can you give me my addictive pleasure?"
My Actions	Go and pay for the addictive desire and use.
My Emotions	Afterwards, I have feelings of guilt, shame, fear, sadness, and anger at myself.

Now, Frances is a positive example of how a surrendered will that seeks to please God (2 Corinthians 5:9) and produce good fruit:

Frances wants to act on her strong desire for her addictive pleasure but she knows it is sinful and wrong. She prays and asks God to help her because

---

[11] Aucoin, Brent, "The Heart of Change," 3 DVD sessions on the message of James 4:1-10, The Faith Resources Counseling Library, www.frlafayette.org, Lafayette, IN.

she knows this desire in her will is wrong. She is saying, "Not my will but yours be done, Lord." Frances reads the Bible and picks one particular verse to memorize to focus her thinking upon what God says and not what she thinks. She devises a plan to carry out God's will for her life. She becomes consumed with accomplishing His will and she does so in word and actions by calling a trusted Christian friend (TCF) and confessing the sinful desires of her heart to God and to her friend. Frances then acts by going to meet her friend for a time of focused prayer and fellowship. Her friend offers more help to Frances, which she gladly accepts.

When Frances comes out of that period of saying "no" to pleasure and "yes" to obeying God, her emotions are lifted high. She realizes that the Holy Spirit has produced His fruit in her heart (Galatians 5:22-23) since she feels loved, joyful, peaceful, patient, and self-controlled. All of these emotions are the result of her obedient choice that began when she denied her will and surrendered to the will of God.

Like Frances in the example above, write out 1 or 2 personal examples from your own experience of how denying your will and obeying His will leads to godly thoughts, words, actions, and eventually emotions.

"for it is God who works in you, both to will and to work for his good pleasure" (Philippians 2:13).

My Will	
God's Will	
My Thoughts	
My Words	
My Actions	
My Emotions	

Example of Frances:

My Will	Addictive Pleasure
God's Will	I want to do what is right in God's eyes.
My Thoughts	I am reading the Word of God to know His thoughts and replace my thoughts with His. Then, I need help and so I will call my friend. I want to obey God more than feel good.
My Words	"Friend, can you help me because I do not want to give in to my addictive pleasure?"
My Actions	Go and meet with my friend for honest fellowship, Bible reading, and prayer. I received love from her and gave her love as well.
My Emotions	Afterwards, I felt loved, joyful, peaceful, patient, and self-controlled and I recognize these are produced by the Holy Spirit inside of me.

When you compare Tommy to Frances, there really is very little difference in how they both desire their own will: the enjoyment of an addictive pleasure. However, rather than allow herself to focus upon that wrong desire, Frances made a decision to fight. She was not passive. She was proactive. She read the Word and prayed. Frances wanted to fight her primary enemy, which was herself—her own will! She surrendered what she wanted to what the Lord wanted and followed it with words and actions that were righteous. Afterwards, she experienced the fruit of the Holy Spirit produced by God. She overcame her one temptation, or "trigger" as the world calls it, but there will be more to come. She must be prepared and plan ahead. Her friend may not be available next time so she must devise a Plan B, because <u>relapse prevention requires more than one plan of escape!</u>

The good news for Tommy is that all of the emotions he felt after his relapse are meant to bring him to his knees in prayer, confession, and repentance of his sin. If Tommy views his willful choice as sinful, then there is hope for him. He can repent and God will forgive him. Maybe the next time Tommy will respond to his temptation, or "trigger," as Frances did in this instance. In time, as both Tommy and Frances practice doing what is right, learning to submit to God's will and resisting the devil (James 4:7), they will develop godly habits that will become more automatic for them. In time and with practice, the temptations to sin will lessen and they will experience more victory and ease in overcoming them.

Emotions are not our enemy. The emotions Tommy experienced—guilt, shame, fear, sadness (or depression), and anger at himself—are meant to be internal alarms that alert us to a bigger problem than just our feelings. Tommy desires the wrong thing (his addictive pleasure) and it is going to destroy him and bring shame to God's name. When Tommy sins, his emotions are going to reflect his wrong choices but they are designed to bring him to a place of brokenness, confession, and repentance before God. God is allowing Tommy's own sin and the feelings that result from that sin to humble him. James 4:9-10 commands this kind of humility: **"Be wretched and mourn and weep. Let your laughter be turned to mourning and your joy to gloom. Humble yourselves before the Lord, and he will exalt you."**

Focus on the emotions you experienced right after your most recent relapse episode. What were some of the feelings you experienced?

Did you recognize those emotions as alarms designed to bring you to your knees in prayer, Bible reading, confession, and repentance?

Relapse prevention requires
_____ _____ _____ _____
_____ _____.

If not, what did you think about the feelings you were experiencing and how did you respond? For example, some people feel guilty and ashamed and take a pill of some type to cover those feelings up. Others turn to "comfort foods" or sex or spending money to cover up their feelings. How did you respond if you failed to see the feelings as alarms to bring you to your knees?

God desires for us to be in right relationship with Him. When we sin, we separate ourselves from Him. When that happens, our emotions get "out of whack" and we start to feel guilt, shame, fear, sadness, anger, or other emotions. One way you can be more aware of your will is to start from your emotions and work backward to your will using the chart below:

My Emotions	My Actions	My Words	My Thoughts	My Will

Use this chart by starting with your emotions and how you were feeling when you sinned or relapsed. Then, think back to your actions and words prior to those emotions. Write those down as well as any thoughts you may remember having prior to the emotions. Finally, analyze what you were really desiring in your will and whether or not it was godly. Sometimes this is hard to do because we deceive ourselves into thinking we are wanting something good.

As you begin working backwards from your emotions, the next step is to learn how to replace your will with God's will. Use the chart below to do the second step of replacing your will with God's will and the thoughts, words, actions, and subsequent fruit of the Spirit that you will experience.

God's Will	My Thoughts	My Words	My Actions	My Emotions

Jeremiah 17:9 reminds us that we have trouble discerning our own will: **"The heart is deceitful above all things, and desperately sick; who can understand it?"** Analyzing your own will is a challenge. We think that most of what we want is righteous in God's eyes, but often we are mistaken. Proverbs 21:2 says: **"Every way of a man is right in his own eyes, but the LORD weighs the heart."** For example, a good desire for a parent is to have a child who obeys him. He may become angry when the child does not obey. The anger may be righteous anger. However, the anger becomes unrighteous when the parent wants the child to obey so much that he is willing to sin to force the child to obey. A strong desire of the will that is NOT submitted to Christ will only lead to ultimate heartache and humiliation no matter what the specific desire is.

Ask yourself: Do I want something too much? Am I willing to sin to get it? Even if it is a biblical desire, you have to understand that your foremost desire must be to please God above all else. Jesus set aside His will as a man to do the will of God in Matthew 26:39b: **"Not as I will, but as You will."**

Do you accept "no" as an answer?

Give a recent example of something that you really wanted but were denied.

"My son, do not despise the LORD's discipline or be weary of his reproof, for the LORD reproves whom he loves as a father the son in whom he delights" (Psalm 3:12-12).

How did you respond to "No, you cannot have that desire"?

How could you have responded to "No" better?

In God's provision, He knows what is best. When He does not allow you to have a desire of your heart, do you trust Him and accept His best for you in that situation?

Read Proverbs 16:9 and write it in the space provided:

What does this verse tell us about our plans and who is ultimately in charge of allowing us to accomplish those plans or not?

If you know that God is loving and good, would you want Him to decide to block your path at times, especially since He knows that the path you would choose would lead to difficulty?

The question really comes down to this: are you going to get angry when you do not get what you want or are you going to trust God and His providence since He loves you?

Write out a brief prayer of trust to God in your own words:

Hebrews 12:11 states: **"For the moment all discipline seems painful rather than pleasant, but later it yields the peaceful fruit of righteousness to those who have been trained by it."** We are all in need of a Savior and transformation to spiritually grow into the likeness of Christ. If you are a child of God, then you will be disciplined as a child but not punished. There is a difference. Punishment is what Jesus experienced on the cross for our sins. Jesus bore our iniquities and our sins as He experienced the just (perfectly fair) wrath of God as punishment. Christians will never experience the wrath of God. Christians will experience discipline from time to time, just as a child receives discipline from a loving parent. The goal is that the child will be trained by that discipline and then produce the peaceful fruit of righteous living. That is God's goal for you, though His discipline may even hurt for a short time period. Mature believers see God's discipline as loving and they accept it (this includes accepting "no" from Him) even when they want something that is good.

"Behold, blessed is the one whom God reproves; therefore despise not the discipline of the Almighty" (Job 5:17).

How has the Lord disciplined you? Give 3 to 5 examples below:

The root word for discipline is "disciple," which is what a Christian is called to become: a disciple of Christ. Sometimes it hurts to be a disciple of Christ because the world rejects you, Satan hates you, and your own flesh is often your enemy. But your flesh requires discipline as you learn to live according to the Holy Spirit within you rather than according to your own pleasures and desires.

What have you learned as a result of His discipline and how can you share it with others?

Chapter Five
How to Fight Temptations or "Triggers"

As human beings, we have appetites. Appetites are "any of the instinctive desires necessary to keep up organic life."[12] These "instinctive desires" are placed in every human being God created. Appetites are internal alarm clocks to remind us that we must do such things as eat, drink, and sleep. When an appetite is satisfied, the satisfaction is only temporary as the appetite will reappear in a short amount of time. Appetites are designed to be satisfied at regular intervals and in moderation to help sustain life.

Appetites should remind us that we are finite, limited, and dependent upon God for our sustenance. We are created to regularly have our *batteries recharged*, so to speak. Appetites are not the cause of the problem for the addict; everyone has appetites but not everyone is addicted. The heart attitudes that drive the habitual, destructive manner in which an addict satisfies instinctive desires are the root of the problem. An addict fulfills appetites by choosing an addictive pleasure excessively, causing a physical dependence, or addiction, to develop. Addiction is not a "disease" but a learned behavior.

It is your _____ _____ that drive the habitual, destructive manner in which you excessively fulfill your addictive desires. "Addiction" is learned behavior and not a _____.

Let's be aware that our appetites are blessings from God intended for regular and moderate, God-glorifying pleasure. It is not a sin for a married couple to have sexual relations every day; however, it *is* a sin for two *unmarried* persons to have sexual relations *any* day according to the Bible. God has given us *protective* parameters in the Bible for fulfilling our natural, God-given desires because He loves us and requires this from us. When we satisfy an appetite in an extreme manner and fail to meet our responsibilities to God, we are committing sin. God sets parameters for our own good to protect us; therefore, if we fulfill an appetite in a manner that is outside of God's protective parameter, there is always danger of physical addiction and its consequences.

In addition to the basic appetites for food, drink, and sex, God has given mankind a spiritual appetite to worship something or someone. "Worship" as a noun is defined as "extravagant respect or admiration for or devotion to an object of esteem."[13] What is the object that pleasurably fulfills your natural appetites, for which you have "extravagant respect and admiration"? What are you prone to devote your thoughts, words, and actions to obtaining? Is it the Lord Jesus Christ or is it an object of temporal value? Christians who have relapsed have a worship problem (called idolatry) in that they seek to fulfill temporary appetites with temporary pleasures rather than disciplining themselves for godliness and eternal rewards. The Apostle Paul told Timothy in 1 Timothy 4:7b-8: **"Rather train yourself for godliness; for while bodily training is of some value, godliness is of value in every way, as it holds promise for the present life and also for the life to come."**

"But each person is tempted when he is lured and enticed by his own desire. Then desire when it has conceived gives birth to sin, and sin when it is fully grown brings forth death" (James 1:14-15).

Christians who have relapsed have a worship problem called _____

---

[12] Merriam-Webster, I. (1996, c1993). *Merriam-Webster's Collegiate Dictionary*. Includes index (10th ed.). Springfield, Mass., U.S.A.: Merriam-Webster.

[13] Ibid.

We must train ourselves to produce godly habits of worshiping our Creator and Sustainer.

What Are Cravings?

Cravings are real, physiological experiences of desire for an addictive pleasure that has been used excessively. The body adapts to the majority of conditions to which it is exposed. Addiction is no different. For example, "tolerance" to alcohol and drugs increases as the substance is increasingly used. This means it takes more and more of the substance to get the same original effect. In particular, the alcohol-addicted person must drink a certain amount of alcohol just to avoid the "shakes," which is a street name for withdrawal symptoms. Addicted people have often declared, "Now, I merely drink alcohol to feel normal." They are telling the truth. This is the physical component of tolerance and cravings, and for this reason, a physician's care is necessary.

For an opiate addict, cravings manifest soon after the effects of the drug cease. Before long, the opiate addict is physically craving the drug again as his or her body has become dependent upon it. Tolerance can be illustrated in the following example:

Suzie takes two or three opiate pills as prescribed by her physician each day for her lower back pain. Over time, the pain in her back still persists after she takes two or three pills, but she finds that by taking five or six pills, the pain disappears. Her body is increasing its tolerance. Suzie's body is saying, "Wow, Suzie keeps getting these opiates in such a great quantity that I (her body) do not have to make any natural endorphins for her anymore. This is great because I can make other things that Suzie needs since she obviously does not need the natural pain relievers that I can make." Suzie now has a problem called "dependence" because she now requires these opiates that come from outside of her body in order to feel "normal."

Cravings are legitimate, diagnostic, and physical phenomena that come from the *excessive* fulfilling of natural appetites. If you are experiencing cravings, you have developed a more serious problem than you realize. Whether you believe you are a "hard core" substance abuser or an "occasional user who sometimes goes to excess," you need God's guidance for living your life in a way that pleases Him. This comes from being self-controlled.

The final fruit of the Spirit discussed in Galatians 5:23 is "self-control." Notice that the object under control is "self." Self is not the *source* of control. Rather, it is the *object* of control. Self is the object that must be controlled.[14] Self must continually remain under the control of the Holy Spirit, not itself.

If you continue to sin by satisfying your natural appetites in excessive and uncontrolled ways, you will develop tolerance, dependence, and cravings. These will become an "inherent" and essential component of

"Better shun the bait than struggle in the snare." John Dryden

When you continue to excessively satisfy your natural appetites, you will develop _____ _____ and _____.

---

[14] This idea was taught to me by Pastor-Teacher Harry Reeder. His sermon series at Briarwood Presbyterian Church, Birmingham, AL (2005) is a great study on the fruit of the Spirit. You may obtain it at www.briarwood.org.

your being. Even if it seems difficult, you must conform your will to God's will. God is not *as* interested in your happiness as He is in your holiness. When you become "holy," you will likely become more joyful. The Bible teaches that your holiness, or obedience, will lead to more joy, happiness, and contentment.

By remaining obedient to God, you will avoid developing insatiable and powerful cravings for your drug of choice. Obedience will enable you to avoid the problems of cravings, dependence, and tolerance. Your biggest problem is not your appetites for alcohol, drugs, sex, sleep, food, or any other addictive pleasure. Instead, it is your sinful heart attitude that prefers to satisfy your appetites with drugs and alcohol rather than with a thriving relationship with an eternal God. Excessive satisfaction of temporary appetites leads to sinful ways of acting, thinking, and speaking that are mental components of addiction. Tolerance, cravings, and dependence upon the addictive pleasure are physical components. Your flesh and its lusts, or strong desires, are your primary problem and your own worst enemy. God's grace will empower you to overcome the addictive tendencies of your heart. His grace is your primary solution!

Nonetheless, you must be aware of what the world calls "triggers" but the Bible calls temptations to sin. Your addictive pleasure is not going to disappear simply because you want it to. The drug dealers do not go away simply because you decide to get clean and sober. Difficult people, situations and temptations will always challenge you. However, you must change how you think about those situations and persons. They may still "trigger" you, or tempt you, by physically causing a reaction in your body. You may see, smell, taste, feel, or hear something that is going to cause your physical body to respond by leading you to want your addictive pleasure very badly.

What the world calls "triggers" is really _____ to _____.

Do you know what "triggers" or tempts you to use? _____ If so, list some of your temptations below:

"For I do not understand my own actions. For I do not do what I want, but I do the very thing I hate (Romans 7:15).

Here is a list of common temptations ("triggers"). Circle those that you think may still tempt you:

- Being around others who are engaging in your addictive pleasure of choice
- Being around others who are talking about your addictive pleasure
- Being around others who are not actively engaging in the addictive pleasure but did so in the past (so it reminds you of your pleasure)

33

- Being isolated and feeling lonely
- Experiencing a temptation but not telling anyone
- Experiencing a temptation and then talking about it in a "fun" way
- Worrying about the past
- Worrying about the future
- Worrying about _____
- Not praying
- Not reading the Bible
- Having too much energy
- Wanting to celebrate something
- Having too little energy, or being tired
- Wanting to sleep, rest, or stay in bed
- Not getting what I want
- Becoming angry when I do not get what I want
- Becoming passive when I do not get what I want; developing an "I don't care" attitude
- Watching tempting programs and commercials on television
- Listening to tempting music
- Taking too much medication
- Not taking enough medication as prescribed by my primary physician
- Not receiving counseling or biblical wisdom from a disciple-maker or trusted Christian friend (TCF)
- Not meeting with my TCF regularly
- Getting prideful
- Thinking I am strong in my own abilities
- Developing a haughty, or prideful, attitude that says I am better than others
- Thinking I am not as bad as others
- Being dishonest with others (spouse, children, TCF, pastor, etc.)
- Telling lies
- Not telling the whole truth (leaving out important details)
- Keeping secrets
- Holding onto hurts
- Being bitter or resentful to those who have hurt or offended me
- Lashing out verbally and/or physically to those who have hurt or offended me
- Talking too much
- Talking too little
- Dreaming of the past (i.e. especially having to do with addiction)
- Dreaming of the future (i.e. especially having to do with addiction)
- Thinking about my own mistakes
- Thinking about my sinful choices too much
- Thinking about sin and evil more than thinking about God and His goodness
- Being irresponsible by missing days at work, school, not doing chores, not coming home, and choosing to procrastinate

- Spending too much time on the computer
- Spending too much time on the phone
- Blaming others for my choices
- Thinking like a victim rather than a responsible person
- Being unthankful
- Being a consumer and wanting to use things for myself, not for others
- Being a taker and not a giver
- Thinking about getting what I deserve
- Thinking about what I did not get that I deserved
- Being mired in self-pity
- Being too proud of my accomplishments
- Being stubborn
- Being rebellious toward God and/or earthly authorities
- Not being humble
- Keeping my addictive pleasure and related paraphernalia around my house or car
- Focusing my thoughts on my addictive pleasure, not God
- Not adjusting well to major changes in my life like the death of a loved one, loss, etc.
- Refusing to deal with problems in my life (avoidance)
- Dealing with problems in my life on my own (too focused on them) and trying to resolve them in my own strength
- Exchanging one addictive pleasure with another one
- Having too much free time (bored)
- Having too little free time (working too much)
- Lacking structure and schedules in my life
- Feeling overwhelmed and stressed out
- Not feeling any urgency about the priorities I need to complete
- Wanting to please people more than pleasing God (Galatians 1:10)
- Stress in a relationship
- Sinning in a relationship and failing to say anything
- Sinning in a relationship and trying to force repentance
- Sinning in my own heart and ignoring it

- Other: _____
- Other: _____
- Other: _____
- Other: _____
- Other: _____
- Other: _____

As you can see, there are many situations that can tempt a person to relapse. Not all of them can be listed. Likely, you listed some of your own temptations that are unique to you. Now, for each one of the above temptations that you circled, write a biblical plan and alternative in the space provided below (see example):

My Temptation	Biblical Alternative	Biblical Plan
I worry about the future.	*The biblical alternative to worry is found in Matthew 6:25-34*	*I will pray and trust God to provide what I need and not look to myself to provide it.*

Now, do this for each one that you circled above. This will take time, but it is important that you do this. Not only do you need to know what "triggers" and tempts you but also what to do about it—what the proper biblical response is that God requires and provides in order for you to overcome it.

Make copies of these two pages or write down your answers on a separate sheet of paper if necessary.

My Temptation	Biblical Alternative	Biblical Plan

My Temptation	Biblical Alternative	Biblical Plan

Chapter Six
Embracing Biblical Terminology:
Coping Skills vs. Put-Ons

There is one problem with the biblical approach to relapse prevention that must be addressed. The problem is that biblical words are different from the world's terminology used in secular counseling. Most people are more familiar with worldly words such as "addiction," "relapse," "alcoholism," "coping skills," "schizophrenia," "manic-depression," "narcissism," and "mental illness" than they are with the biblical terminology in the put-off/ put-on principle in Ephesians 4:20-24. Biblical words such as "sin," "pride," "drunkenness," and "idolatry" are not socially acceptable any more. If you were to look up the worldly terms listed above in your Bible, you would not find them.

Circle the terms that are biblical:
Drunkenness
Narcissism
Addiction
Manic-Depression
Adultery
Idolatry

So, does that mean that the Bible is irrelevant? Does it mean that the Bible is silent on these issues that the world has labeled as "addiction", "mental illness", "alcoholism" and the like? The answer is "no," because the Bible does address these issues but uses different language (see Appendix C for a comparison and contrast of worldly ideas and biblical principles). A TCF or good biblical counselor will be a "translator" to help you to better understand the biblical principles that address your thoughts, words, and actions without turning to worldly terminology to describe it.

Coping Skills or Put-ons

One example that demonstrates the difference between worldly ideas and biblical principles is illustrated in the comparison between a coping skill and a "put-on." The worldly term "coping skill" is an action phrase meant to help people. In fact, worldly thinking divides these actions into two categories: "positive coping mechanisms" and "negative coping mechanisms" based upon whether they help the person or not. The Bible's replacement for "coping skill" is simple and practical because it will both benefit the person and glorify the Lord when it is implemented. The biblical idea of a "coping skill" is called a "put-on" in Ephesians 4:24: **"and to put on the new self, created after the likeness of God in true righteousness and holiness."** A "put-on" is a new thought, word, or action that is like Christ and is right, true, and pure. Ask your TCF or biblical counselor to help you develop a list of biblical put-ons with a heart that seeks to glorify God.

"You must teach what is in accord with sound doctrine" (Titus 2:1, NIV).

In the secular world, coping negatively includes any addiction like cutting, self-injurious behavior, gambling, drug addiction, drinking coffee excessively, smoking cigarettes, eating "comfort" foods, drinking alcohol, and the like. These are "learned behaviors" to which people turn to find comfort that end up hurting them more in the long run. The Bible teaches

The best coping skill is Romans 12:2: "Do not be conformed to this world, but be transformed by the renewal of your mind…"

that turning to anything or anyone other than Christ will not satisfy the desires in your heart. Thus, negative coping skills might relieve emotional pain temporarily but will not provide any eternal benefit and will likely have negative consequences in this temporary life you are living on earth.

Secular coping skills are "positive" when you employ actions such as listening to music, drawing pictures, watching movies, playing video games, drawing a butterfly on the area where you are tempted to cut yourself, yoga, meditation, exercising, seeing a therapist, calling a friend, taking a shower or bath, or owning a pet. While some of these things are not sinful or wrong, they tend to focus ONLY upon a personal benefit, which is only half of God's purpose for you according to 1 Corinthians 10:31: **"So, whether you eat or drink, or whatever you do, do all to the glory of God."**

List some "negative coping skills" that have led you into addictive thinking and actions.

What are some "positive" yet biblical ways in which you could have handled your situations and circumstances.

Putting on so-called positive coping skills should benefit you but ultimately bring _____ to God.

You are created to glorify God in what you think, speak, and do, so the goal of "fixing yourself" is only half of the goal God sets for you. God's objective for His children is for them to be conformed to the image of His son. You must learn to "put-on" so-called "positive" coping skills that are Christ-like and will ultimately bring Him glory. Such put-ons reflect the motives in your heart because **whether you eat or drink, or whatever you do,** you are to do it for **the glory of God** (1 Corithians 10:31). For example, if you choose the world's "positive" coping skill of drawing pictures that are violent, murderous, or sexual, then that would not be to the glory of God since He forbids such things in His Word of truth (Exodus 20, 3 John 1:11 and Philippians 4:8). The biblical put-on would be to draw pictures that reflect the loving character of God and not the sin of the world.

The blessing in choosing a biblical "put-on" is that whatever you choose to do for the glory of God will also benefit others, if what you are doing is godly according to the Word of God. Seek to glorify Him and help others in your thoughts, words, and actions as biblical put-ons that are acceptable "coping skills" in God's eyes. If you can answer the question, "Am I doing _____ for the glory of God?" with a clear conscience, then do the action that fills in the blank space above.

Choose Your Words Carefully

Biblical principles and words point us to sin and our need for a Savior. Worldly ideas and words point us toward so-called mental illness "disease," mental disorders, and psychological problems devoid of God and often directing the attention to physical manifestations alone. While some "psychological" problems can be physical in nature, the majority of them are caused either by sinful choices or by wrong responses to being sinned against by others. Biblical language rightly defines the responsibility of mankind toward God for our sin and for our reaction to being sinned against.

Ultimately, every problem in our lives goes back to the sin of our first parents, Adam and Eve, who willingly chose to disobey God's Word. They did not trust God at His Word and we have the same problem today. Do you trust God enough to obey His commands? You are encouraged to look at the sin in your own life, to confess it, and to turn from it (Proverbs 28:13), so that you might turn back to God who loves you and created you for His good pleasure, that you might learn to think, speak, and act more like Jesus (Romans 8:29). Ephesians 2:10 reminds us: **"For we are his workmanship, created in Christ Jesus for good works, which God prepared beforehand, that we should walk in them."** The Lord wants you to "put-on" new ways of thinking, speaking, and doing for His glory and your benefit both.

> Using biblical words and terms instead of worldly terms point us to our _____ and our need for a _____.

What is Sin?

Sin is not only what you are doing that is wrong but also includes what you are *failing* to do! For example, a young, newly married husband may be hanging out with his buddies, playing video games or cards with them, and not *doing* anything wrong according to the Bible. However, in this case, it is not what he is doing but what he is *failing* to do that may be causing the problems in his marriage when his wife feels neglected, unappreciated, and unloved. This husband is failing to love his wife according to Ephesians 5:28 and a good biblical counselor will point out his sin of omission. His wife may respond to his sin of omission with her own sinful choice to withhold affection and to use harsh words (Ephesians 4:29). Her response to his sin is called a sin of commission in that she is outright committing a sin. As you can see, both types of sin cause reactions, heartache, separation, and other negative consequences. Sin always brings separation and distrust between people and between those people and the Lord.

> "Anything that comes between me and God is an idol—anything!" D.L. Moody

The Lord has provided biblical counseling so that you might learn His thoughts as revealed in His Word (the Bible) and make right choices in your life that are pleasing to Him. God knows that the best way for you to live is to be surrendered to Him and His plan for your life. Proverbs 3:5 tells us NOT to trust in ourselves, our own perceptions, or our own understanding based upon what we have learned from the world, but to **"trust in the LORD**

Sin by any other name is—still sin.

with all your heart, and do not lean on your own understanding." The Lord wants you to know Him better so that you can trust Him more and walk by faith. He will reveal Himself to you as you study, read, meditate, obey, and memorize His Word of truth. For this reason, you must embrace biblical terminology more than you do worldly terminology and, in some instances, you may need to reject worldly thinking altogether. Do so primarily because you want to become closer to God in your relationship with Him, and He will draw Himself closer to you (James 4:8).

Conclusion

The Lord has more in store for you than just "coping" with life and developing skills to help you feel better. He wants you to feel better but for the right reason. He wants you to live your life for Him: **"For whoever would save his life will lose it, but whoever loses his life for my sake will save it"** (Luke 9:24, Matthew 16:25, Mark 8:35). You will lose your old life, but you will find new life in Christ as you develop godly habits, according to the put-off and put-on principle of Ephesians 4:20-24, require daily practice and discipline (1 Timothy 4:7). God promises you will be a new creation in Christ in 2 Corinthians 5:17: **"Therefore, if anyone is in Christ, he is a new creation. The old has passed away; behold, the new has come."**

Chapter Seven

Walking in Newness of Life: Godly Habits

The key to bringing about lasting change and preventing a relapse in the future is for develop godly habits by the power of the Holy Spirit. The Lord has provided for His children a powerful principle found in Scripture that will transform your life. This profound principle is so simple that many Christians miss it!

> **But that is not the way you learned Christ!— assuming that you have heard about him and were taught in him, as the truth is in Jesus, to put off your old self, which belongs to your former manner of life and is corrupt through deceitful desires, and to be renewed in the spirit of your minds, and to put on the new self, created after the likeness of God in true righteousness and holiness** (Ephesians 4:20-24).

"I will give them a heart to know that I am the LORD, and they shall be my people and I will be their God, for they shall return to me with their whole heart (Jeremiah 24:7).

This passage of Scripture is written to Christians who have learned the way and truth about Christ. Their goal is to become like Him, but this is going to require four things.

1. Learn who Christ is and what He stands for (verse 20-21 above). You do this by reading the Bible, being mentored by a trusted Christian friend (TCF), listening to solid Bible teaching, and learning about God as you walk with Him throughout your lifetime. You learn about Christ by learning the truth of God's Word **"as the truth is in Jesus."** In this sense, it is really pretty simple: read the Bible and ask the Holy Spirit to enlighten you to see who Jesus is and how you can become like Him. The Holy Spirit works in partnership with the Word of God, so do not limit His work in your life by not reading the Bible.

2. The person who becomes a Christ follower must put off, or cast off, the old manner of life, since it is corrupted and polluted through deceitful desires of the will (verse 22 above). Think about taking off your work clothes so that you can put on your evening clothes.

3. After you put off your old self and its deceitful, corrupted desires, you must ask the Holy Spirit to renew the attitude of your mind (verse 23 above). Quite simply, you must want God to make you hate what you once loved and love what you once hated or despised. Only God can change an attitude and it will only occur in a willing, surrendered person.

4. When you have put off your old desires and been renewed in your attitude, you must put on the new self which will resemble Jesus Christ and involve righteous choices (verse 24 above). Not only do you take off your old clothing, but you put on new clothing. God wants to clothe you in the righteous robe of Christ.

"But put on the Lord Jesus Christ, and make no provision for the flesh to gratify its desires (Romans 13:14).

So yes, you have some work to do, but God gives you the desire to obey His Word and the power and ability to do His will by the Holy Spirit (Philippians 2:13). God will transform you and grow you spiritually as you continue to practice doing these four things:

1. Learn the truth which is in Jesus.
2. Put off your old desires.
3. Ask the Holy Spirit to renew (or change) your mind and your attitudes.
4. Put on new, righteous thoughts, words, and actions so that you become a new, transformed person.

When you begin doing these things, you will become more like Christ. Christ was humble, not prideful. Christ was meek, not sinfully angry or out of control. Christ was giving, not selfish. Christ was thankful to the Father, not bitter or discontent. In other words, your new self will look nothing like your old self.

Habits

God has given all human beings the ability to save time by creating good habits. Brushing your teeth is a discipline you learned as a child. Now you do it without thinking. You save time by not having to relearn the process each time you do it. Buckling your seatbelt before starting your vehicle is a habit that might save your life. Habits become automatic.

The world says bad habits must be broken. Scripture says they must be _____.

The problem is that most of us have learned very bad habits that harm us. Bad habits only lead to heartache when they lead us to sin without thinking. When sin becomes so habitual that it looks automatic, relapse will become too easy.

Habits are not just a physical component of addiction, they also involve a mental component: thoughts. Habits can be formed in your thoughts, words, and actions. Everyone is a creature of habit. Habits are not designed to be "broken" as the world believes. Instead, according to God's Truth, habits must be replaced. Poor habits must be and can be replaced by good habits. It is not sufficient for the cigarette smoker to simply quit smoking by "breaking the habit" after "detoxing" from the physical dependence of nicotine. The cigarette smoker must also replace smoking cigarettes with something constructive that glorifies God. In the Bible, this is called "putting off" and "putting on" and it can be applied to many areas of your life. Every Christian addict is capable of replacing sinful habits of thinking and behaving with godly habits.

"It isn't that they can't see the solution. It is that they can't see the problem." G.K. Chesterton

What habits do you have in thoughts, words, or actions that you need to replace with godly ones?

With what new habits can you replace each of the habits listed above?

How must your mind be renewed (or changed and transformed) for each habit you listed in the first set above? For example, "I love chocolate, but now I must think of chocolate as potentially harmful to me and eat it only once per week." Be specific.

"Addiction" is redefined as the persistent _____ use of a substance known by the user to be _____.

Secular, worldly thinking describes addiction as a "disease" and uses the word "compulsive" to describe what is really a sinful choice. "I cannot stop it because it is compulsive" is what you might hear people say. They believe they cannot help their addiction. However, rather than addiction being "compulsive," it is really "habitual," so if you eliminate the word "compulsive" from the worldly definition for "addiction" and replace it with "habitual," then "addiction" becomes a word that aligns with Scripture. In *The Heart of Addiction*, "addiction" is redefined as the "persistent habitual use of a substance known by the user to be harmful." While the word "addiction" was created by the world, this new definition transforms addiction into a word more closely resembling the life-devastating sin of drunkenness described in the Bible. This new definition of addiction brings more hope to the suffering, relapsing Christian addict. There is hope because ungodly, destructive habits can be replaced by godly, productive habits. Real and lasting change can and will occur in your life.

Therefore, I urge you to heed the warning of Colossians 2:8: **"See to it that no one takes you captive by philosophy and empty deceit, according to human tradition, according to the elemental spirits of the world, and not according to Christ."** Think about addiction with biblical principles and understand that you are a creature of habit. God has plenty to say about addictive thoughts, habits, and behaviors. He has designed you and created you to be a creature of habit, but it is not His design for you to go to extremes when attempting to satisfy your natural appetites and desires.

Physical addiction occurs when you _____ satisfy a natural appetite and desire with a temporary _____ until you become the _____ of it instead of its _____.

Quite simply, physical addiction occurs when you repeatedly satisfy a natural appetite or desire with a temporary pleasure until you become the servant of it rather than its master. Addiction is likened to slavery, adultery, and idolatry in the Bible. You use the temporary, pleasurable substance or activity to escape, but in reality you find that you are physically and emotionally enslaved rather than free. Human beings love a pleasurable "escape" because it seems so freeing, but addiction is a trap that lets you think that you will be "free" when, in reality, you become a "slave." God created you to have liberty in Christ, but that freedom from the slavery of sin was not without cost. It cost the Son of God His life on the cross.

How has your addiction enslaved you? List 3 to 5 personal examples with specific details.

The Bible teaches that we, as Christians, are to present ourselves to God for righteousness. This will empower us to say "no" to giving ourselves over to sinful desires in the old habits of the flesh while saying "yes" to obeying God and doing what is right. We are to see ourselves as God's property. When we belong to Him, our will must become God's will; He is our Master. You may not like the idea of belonging to God and being owned by Him as a Master, but remember that God cares for you more than you even love yourself! In reality, people are going to be slaves either to sin or to righteousness unto God, according to Romans 6:16-19:

> **Do you not know that if you present yourselves to anyone as obedient slaves, you are slaves of the one whom you obey, either of sin, which leads to death, or of obedience, which leads to righteousness? But thanks be to God, that you who were once slaves of sin have become obedient from the heart to the standard of teaching to which you were committed, and, having been set free from sin, have become slaves of righteousness. I am speaking in human terms, because of your natural limitations. For just as you once presented your members as slaves to impurity and to lawlessness leading to more lawlessness, so now present your members as slaves to righteousness leading to sanctification.**

You are to present your body as a surrendered soul (consider yourself a slave belonging to God). You are to do what is right in God's eyes, practicing godly habits in the sanctification[15] process of "putting on." You are to work at becoming "godly," or more like Christ, so that your good, righteous habits become second nature to you. For example, actions of love must become automatic to you. Maybe you have learned to spend time talking with your wife each evening after dinner rather than watching television. You have put off time watching TV and have put on spending time with your wife. As you practice this loving act of listening to your wife, it should become habitual in a good way. Most Christians do not think of godliness as something to be practiced, but as 1 Timothy 4:7b-8 states: **"Rather train yourself for godliness; for while bodily training is of some value, godliness is of value in every way, as it holds promise for the present life and also for the life to come."** In other words, godliness (exemplified in the loving actions of a husband toward a wife, for example) is not natural; it requires training, and must be practiced. Good habits are developed intentionally.

For those who struggle with relapse, ungodliness and selfishness have been practiced for so long that change seems like an unattainable goal. It

"No man can serve two masters, for either he will hate the one and love the other, or he will be devoted to the one and despise the other. You cannot serve both God and money" (the flesh) *(Matthew 6: 24).*

---

[15] Sanctification is a biblical term meaning growing and increasing in Christ-likeness in our hearts and actions.

may seem as unattainable as running a marathon would be for a "couch potato," or someone who is overweight. Nonetheless, just as running a marathon requires self-denial, discipline and training, godliness requires self-denial, discipline and training. The prize is well worth the training as it profits both in this life and in the eternal life to come according to 1 Timothy 4:8. No one gets up from the couch and runs 26 miles without the daily, weekly, and monthly discipline of training, exercising, and running a few miles every day. After time, the marathon becomes possible through practice and daily discipline.

Running a marathon and godliness both require the same things:
———————————
———————————
———————————.

Make some goals now to become a more Christ-like person. Choose one area to work on (i.e. be more trusting of the Lord, know God more, be more peaceful, be more joyful, be more patient, be more kind, etc. See Galatians 5:22-23 for more examples). Be specific as to how you can improve this area of your character on a daily, weekly, and monthly basis:

Example of a Goal: I want to become more kind to others.
Daily: I am going to smile and say encouraging comments to my family today.
Weekly: I am going to memorize Philippians 4:8 and practice it daily for a week.
Monthly: I am going to intentionally pray for my family and especially for those who are "mean" to me this month.

Your Goal:

Daily:

Weekly:

Monthly:

"The object of your faith must be Christ, not faith in ritual, not faith in sacrifice, not faith in morals, not faith in yourself—not in anything but Christ." Billy Graham

Hint: I suggest that you pick one goal to work on each month. The fruit of the Spirit in Galatians 5:22-23 will give you ideas to help you to focus upon one area.

Renewing Your Mind

So, is replacing a bad habit with a good habit enough? Not according to our passage of Scripture in Ephesians 4:20-24. We must experience a renewing of our mind. I call this the "Holy Spirit" step of the process of change because only God can change our heart desires. We cannot even change our own hearts! God must do that work in us. Philippians 2:13 affirms this: **"for it is God who works in you, both to will and to work for his good pleasure."**

"If you keep my commandments, you will abide in my love, just as I have kept my Father's commandments and abide in his love" (John 15:10).

Detoxification and the "putting off" of old habits are not enough. It is not enough to simply "put on" new habits either. There must be a mind renewal, mind change, or mind transformation. (Review Chapter 3.) Some call this an "attitude adjustment," but it is much stronger than that! Ephesians 4:23 places mind renewal right between the "putting off" and "putting on" of the biblical change of habits: **"to be renewed in the spirit of your minds."**

"Saturate your mind with Scripture and the Holy Spirit will give you the ability to discern good from evil so that you make godly choices that glorify Christ."
Mark Shaw

How do you renew your mind? You do it when you place the _____ of God in your _____.

Romans 12:2 emphasizes that the transformation begins in one's thinking and leads to a person being able to discern the will of God: **"Do not be conformed to this world, but be transformed by the renewal of your mind, that by testing you may discern what is the will of God, what is good and acceptable and perfect."** Think about the implication of this verse: change the way you think by becoming more biblical in your thoughts and you will be able to better discern God's will, not your own will! Does not every Christian, especially one who struggles with addiction, need to implement this principle? The answer is a resounding yes!

If mind renewal does not happen, you will fail. Eventually, you will relapse if your mind is NOT renewed ("renewed" really means "changed" and is similar to the word "repentance," which means a "change of mind leading to a change in actions"). For example, think about the thousands of people who have *completely* overcome the physical withdrawal symptoms of a substance, only to find themselves enslaved to the very same substance again later in their lives. Detoxification from a substance alone is not enough. Something new has to replace the old, and a new desire has to be placed in the heart of the person by the Holy Spirit to renew the mind, bringing about Christ-likeness.

How do you renew your mind? You don't do it alone, but God does it when you place the Word of God inside your heart. In other words, you are 100% responsible for your part and God is 100% responsible for His part and I guarantee you that He will deliver!

Colossians 3:16 states: **"Let the word of Christ dwell in you richly, teaching and admonishing one another in all wisdom, singing psalms and hymns and spiritual songs, with thankfulness in your hearts to God."** Let God's Word take up residence inside of you so much that it permeates all that you do and say.

Let's look at one way you can study God's Word, meditate on and memorize it so that your mind may be renewed by the Holy Spirit:

1. Before reading the passage, pray that God would open your eyes so that you can see clearly the lies you have believed and the truth that you must believe.
2. Read the passage one time through without stopping.
3. Read the passage again slowly and break it up into smaller phrases/words/pieces so that you can gain an understanding of each piece separately.
4. Think about what God's message is communicating to you in each separate piece.
5. Meditate upon each phrase until you have a better understanding of that section.
6. Memorize the verse by writing down the piece of Scripture and stating it out loud over and over.
7. Close your eyes and see if you can recite it without looking.

8. Now, move to the next piece of the Scripture verse and repeat steps 4-7 above.

9. At the end, recite the entire verse together and practice it three times per day (breakfast, lunch, and dinner) so that you have it down perfectly, smoothly, and quickly.

10. State it to a trusted Christian friend or loved one. Tell them what it means and how it helped you.

Now let's try it with the following passage:

But that is not the way you learned Christ!— assuming that you have heard about him and were taught in him, as the truth is in Jesus, to put off your old self, which belongs to your former manner of life and is corrupt through deceitful desires, and to be renewed in the spirit of your minds, and to put on the new self, created after the likeness of God in true righteousness and holiness (Ephesians 4:20-24).

"I appeal to you therefore, brothers, by the mercies of God, to present your bodies as a living sacrifice, holy and acceptable to God, which is your spiritual worship" (Romans 12:1).

1. Pray: "Lord, please open my eyes so that I might see what I need to do to change and how you are going to change me at the same time. I want to see wonderful things in your law today" (Psalm 119:18).

2. Read it through one time.

3. Now, read it slowly. Although I would break it up in this manner, you can break it up into even more pieces than this:

   a. But that is not the way you learned Christ
   b. assuming that you have heard about him
   c. and were taught in him
   d. as the truth is in Jesus
   e. to put off your old self
   f. which belongs to your former manner of life
   g. and is corrupt through deceitful desires
   h. and to be renewed in the spirit of your minds
   i. and to put on the new self
   j. created after the likeness of God in true righteousness and holiness.

4. God is stating the following: (Letters correspond to verse breakdown above.)

   • I must evaluate how I have learned Christ (a).

   • Do I really know Him? (b).

   • Have I been taught accurately who He is? (c).

   • The truth is in Christ Jesus (d).

   • I must change. **The lie I believed** is that I could go on living irresponsibly and keep drinking, "drugging" and living selfishly without consequences. The truth is that I must put off my old way of doing things (e,f,g).

- My old self is that person who is selfish and lives like the unbeliever that I used to be. **The lie I believed** is that I can live like an addict and still claim to be living like a Christian. The truth is that my lifestyle as an addict is not glorifying to God because it reflects the life of an unbeliever rather than the life of a Christian (e,f,g,h).

- I need to be renewed in the spirit of my mind. I need to think biblically. **The lie I believed** is that I can stop doing drugs (alcohol, overeating or whatever) on my own (put-off) without having to do anything else. The truth is that I must have my mind renewed about God, addiction, others, and myself. The battle begins in my mind and my thinking leads to emotions and actions (g,h,i,j).

- I must put-on a new self. I must become a new person. **The lie I believed** is that I can never change. If I stop doing drugs and do nothing else, then I am still a drug addict and drunkard even though I am not using (called a "dry drunk" in secular world). Therefore, the truth is that I must begin to think and act like a new creation in Christ by glorifying God in my actions. I must do things for others and consider others more important than myself (h,i,j).

- Wow. I have been created by God and after His likeness, so how did I get into this sinful mess of addiction? I do not act righteously or holy when I am in the midst of my addiction. **The lie I believed** is that I am a piece of junk that God created by mistake. The truth is that I am His creation, and I can act rightly by the power of the Holy Spirit (a-j).

5. Christian meditation is different from secular meditation (i.e. yoga, etc.). Christians actively think about a specific verse or passage of Scripture and how it applies to their lives. Secular meditation is passive. In it you may allow anything and everything to come into your mind. There is no direction or focus. "Freedom" is encouraged, but what comes into your mind is often not "freeing" at all! Christians must be purposeful and active in their thought life; therefore, meditation for the Christian is ALWAYS upon the pure truths found in the Word of God. Meditate upon the verse or passage of Scripture each day for a week.

6. Memorize each piece of the above verse and slowly join it together as a cohesive unit. For this particular passage, I would take my time and spend at least a week on it.

7. Close your eyes and recite it piece by piece at first. Then, try to do the entire passage. Take your time. This is not a race!

8. Practice the piece that you are working on before each meal. Or speak the piece during the prayer for your meal. Be creative!

9. Ask your spouse, friend, or family member if you can recite it for them. This will encourage them as well as you. Do not be afraid of failing or "looking foolish." Honor God.

10. Try this same exercise with your own selected passages or use the following:

Genesis 3 or 4	John 14, 15, 16, or 17
Psalms 10, 23, 37, 51, and 149	Galatians 5 or 6
Proverbs 3:5-8	Ephesians 4, 5, or 6
Micah 6:6-8	Philippians 1:18-30, 2, or 3
Matthew 5, 6, or 7	Colossians 3 or 4
Luke 10, 11, or 12	

After having your mind renewed by the Holy Spirit and putting off old habits, you must be diligent to replace the old habits with new habits that are Christ-like. This is called "putting on," according to Ephesians 4:24.

Below are sample "put off" and "put on" lists. You may start with these lists as you begin developing your own lists for your life. Some of these are things that you may not have considered. Remember that you can add anything you want to "put on" as long as it is not sinful and will glorify the Lord.

THINGS TO PUT OFF:

WHAT
- Clothes advertising alcohol and drugs.
- Cell phones. Too tempting and not needed.
- Cigarettes. Believe it or not, those who give up smoking improve their ability to stay clean and sober.
- Coolers used to keep alcoholic drinks cold.
- Cars. There may be situations in which you need to limit your freedom. No need to drive for a few months. Ask for rides to work. Humble yourself.
- Secular books and magazines. You know what to read instead (… starts with a "B")
- Television. Too many beer commercials glamorizing the drunkard's lifestyle.
- Internet. Too many temptations to do wrong.

Add your own specific things:

WHERE
- Bars and restaurants where you used to "hang out" and drink/drug.
- Houses of old "using buddies," friends, and "drinking buddies."
- Convenience stores. Too tempting and too easy to pick up alcohol.
- Grocery store liquor and beer aisles. As you grocery shop just avoid that particular aisle. Do not even look toward the aisle. Look away and focus on other places in the store when you see that aisle.

- Houses of friends and relatives who drink (may be necessary for only 6 months or so). Avoid temptation.
- Places, houses, neighborhoods, and streets where you used to buy drugs and alcohol. Drive a different route if necessary.
- Avoid your place of purchase at all costs and especially if you are alone.

Add your own specific places:

WHO
- Some relationships must be put-off permanently while other relationships may only require a temporary put-off.
- Avoid old "using buddies" and "friends" permanently.
- Avoid dealers and shady acquaintances at all costs.
- Avoid meeting new people alone. Have a friend or relative with you.
- Some relatives may have to be put-off permanently if they drink/ drug. Friends, too.
- Some relatives who drink may be put-off temporarily until you can confide in them and ask them to help you with your struggles.
- If single, relationships with the opposite sex often need to be put-off.
- Co-workers who encourage drinking and drugging. Do not associate intimately with them while at work and especially after work hours in a social setting.

Add your own specific people:

WHEN
- Put-off being alone for long periods of time (an hour may be too long to some while 30 minutes is too long for others).
- Put-off feelings of hurt and rejection by going to the person who hurt you directly in order to reconcile the relationship.
- For the first major holidays when you are sober, consider putting-off where you used to spend your holidays so that you can create a new tradition somewhere else, if necessary.

Add your own specific times:

WHY
- Perishing mentality must be put-off as it contributes to depression, hopelessness, anger, self-pity, etc.
- Do not allow yourself to become a pessimist only. You must become balanced.

Add your own specific reasons:

THINGS TO PUT ON

WHAT
- Clothes advertising Jesus Christ, your church, and Bible verses.
- Meet in person with an elder, deacon, or mature Christian. Coffee or lunch if you like.
- Chew gum.
- Put a pocket sized Bible in the exact place where you carried your cigarettes. They are about the same size so it is a great substitute. Read it when you have a physical craving to smoke.
- Keep a box of Christian CDs, evangelistic tracts, and books in your car where you kept your cooler for cold beer! Fill your mp3 player or other digital music device with Christian music!
- Walk. Exercise is so good for the transforming Christian addict. Check with your physician first!
- Christian books and magazines. The Bible.
- Read a book instead of watching TV. Write your own book based on Scriptures and your life story.
- Spend the time you would have spent on the internet or watching TV in a real conversation—face-to-face fellowship with another Christian believer. Have a real relationship with someone and focus upon helping them in some way.
- Females: Make a meal for someone else and bring it to them.
- Males: Offer a friend help or service without expecting anything in return.
- Drink lots of water to replace your physiological thirst and desires for alcohol. Always have something you can be drinking like water, juice, or healthy, non-alcoholic drinks. Experiment and find tasteful, new healthy drinks that you have not tried before.
- Fresh fruits and vegetables. Try some you have never tried before!

Add your own specific things:

WHERE

- Church, Bible studies, and fellowship meetings with other Christians must be your new "hang out."
- Invite Christians into your home for fun, fellowship, prayer, or Bible study.
- Gas up at the pump rather than going into the convenience store. Obtain a prepaid card if you don't have credit.
- Think about the aisles you *can* walk down rather than focusing upon the one aisle you must avoid. Look at the things you *can* buy and enjoy moderately while at the store.
- Clearly instruct friends and relatives who drink that they cannot bring alcohol when coming to your house.
- Plan out a different route to drive home to avoid places, houses, neighborhoods, and streets where you used to buy drugs and alcohol.

Add your own specific places:

WHO

- You must put-on relationships that are godly and drug free. Since some relationships must be put-off permanently while other relationships may only require a temporary put-off, be sure to intentionally add relationships with a permanent mindset; however, it may only be temporary, as time will tell.
- Get an accountability partner who can speak the truth in love to you.
- Get a pastor, elder, or deacon who can be your Bible-teaching "dealer" rather than visiting a drug dealer!
- Meet new people only when you have a friend or relative with you.
- Call relatives that you may have avoided in the past because you considered them to be "goody-two-shoes" or "holier-than-thou" types who did not approve of your partying. These very relatives may become your best relationships.
- Ask relatives who are Christians to help you by praying for you and calling you and encouraging you to stay sober. Humble yourself and confide in them but use good judgment because not everyone can keep from gossiping.
- If single, cultivate friendships with the same gender for now rather than seeking the approval of the opposite sex.
- Hang out with co-workers who encourage Christian living and morals. Associate with them while at work and after work hours in a social setting, but only if allowed by your employer's rules.

Add your own specific people:

WHEN

- Put-on being alone with God for periods of time in prayer and Bible reading.
- Put-on spending time with other Christian believers for times of fellowship and encouragement.
- Put-on intentionally and lovingly going to someone when he hurts you in order to reconcile the relationship. Be meek, humble, and loving, considering how much you have sinned and been forgiven of by God (Ephesians 4:32, Matthew 18).
- Fill your most tempting time of the day with a special plan to focus upon helping others and studying and worshipping God (i.e. time of day, seasons, holidays, etc.).

Add your own specific times:

WHY

- Joyful mentality must be put-on regardless of your circumstances, trials, problems, and adverse situations. Count it all joy (James 1:2). Also, read Romans 8:28-29.
- Become balanced in your pessimism (or realism as you probably call it) and be an optimist, too! Again, Romans 8:28-29 comes to mind!
- Develop a gratitude list, or a think list, based upon Philippians 4:8-9.[16]

"Holiness is like a seed sown into the ground. It grows gradually into a plant."

John Owen

Add your own specific reasons:

The put off and put on dynamic is a powerful principle in Scripture that is easily understood but hard to do since it requires discipline. The discipline comes in the form of learning Christ through reading the Word of God, and mind renewal through the transforming power of the Holy Spirit. As you seek to change, you will no longer be what you once were. Those who daily confess the words "I am an addict" are reminding themselves of their sin, and although this can be good to remain humble, it would be better to proclaim your new identity as no longer tied to your sin but to Christ. If it is true you can say, "I am a redeemed sinner and follower of Christ," if you are indeed being transformed by His grace.

---

[16] Adams, Jay, *The Christian Counselor's New Testament*, Hackettstown, NJ: Timeless Texts, p. 613.

Chapter Eight
A New Way to Be Human

After learning about Christ, putting off old habits, being renewed in your mind by the Holy Spirit, and then putting on new habits that are Christ-like, you are now ready for a new way to be human. You are ready to be Spirit-led as you yield your will to the Holy Spirit's will. What a way to live! It is exciting, challenging, and fulfilling both in this life and in the eternal life to come.

To prevent relapse, you must adopt God's mind. You must think thoughts that are like His thoughts. Sadly, there are five very dangerous mindsets in addictive thinking that lead to patterns of living for self. Someone who is in an active addiction is labeled an "addict," but he is actually a person who is focused upon pleasing self and willing to sin to do so. As the word "addict" has been used in this workbook, it is descriptive of a self-centered person caught in a physical trap of addiction.

So how does an addict think and act? An addict is living to please himself and is fulfilling the desires of his own "flesh." When I begin biblically counseling someone coming out of active "addiction," I can count on the person thinking in *five* particular ways: an entitlement mentality, a consumer mentality, a victim mentality, a perishing mentality, and a rebellious mentality. I call these "mentalities" because they are a predominant way of thinking about life. A "mentality" is defined as a "mode or way of thought" that affects one's outlook on life.[17] It is a view of the world that colors the perceptions of a person and leads to interpretations of the world consistent with that view.

List the five mentalities that are characteristic of "addictive" thinking:

1.

2.

3.

4.

5.

What is interesting about these five mentalities is that each one builds upon the previous mentality. If you observe an "addict" you will begin to see the "entitlement" and "consumer" mentalities manifest. The addict begins thinking he deserves better than what he is receiving (entitlement) and he consumes whatever he has upon himself (consumer). Next you will see a "victim" mentality begin to emerge. The addict is now thinking that he is a "victim" of neglect or unfair treatment when a family member or friend does not give him his every desire. Note that the addict feels entitled and lives like a consumer; therefore, unmet desires frustrate him because he is living to please himself but is unable to do so. Rather than blame himself, he blames God, family members, parents, friends, and others! Family members are perceived as harsh because the addict has an "entitlement" and "consumer" mentality.

Next, the addict who is now thinking like a "victim" will develop a "perishing mentality." This new mindset is mired in self-pity, focusing his thoughts too much on himself in terms of what he does not have: "Bad things always happen to me." This attitude is actually a lack of gratitude that leads to despondent thinking, feeling sorry for oneself, and self-destructive

The "victim" mentality is mired in _____-_____.

---

[17] Merriam-Webster, I. (1996, c1993). *Merriam-Webster's Collegiate Dictionary.* Includes index (10th ed.). Springfield, Mass., U.S.A.: Merriam-Webster.

actions. In the final stage, the addict who now thinks with a "perishing mentality" begins thinking and acting like a rebel. "Why should I try to do right or please anybody or even please God?" says the addict who manifests the "rebellious" mentality. The end result is a rebellious, angry, and foolish-acting person who seeks to be independent—to to be free from any rules, laws, or restrictions. The addict wants to be his own boss at all costs.

These mentalities are understood clearly in light of the following two passages of Scriptures:

> **And He said to him, "You shall love the Lord your God with all your heart and with all your soul and with all your mind** (opposite of entitlement). **This is the great and first commandment. And a second is like it: You shall love your neighbor as yourself** (opposite of consumer). **On these two commandments depend all the Law and the Prophets"** (Matthew 22:37-40).

> **And do not get drunk with wine, for that is debauchery, but be filled with the Spirit,** (opposite of victim) **addressing one another in psalms and hymns and spiritual songs, singing and making melody to the Lord with all your heart, giving thanks always and for everything to God the Father in the name of our Lord Jesus Christ** (opposite of perishing), **submitting to one another out of reverence for Christ** (opposite of rebellious) (Ephesians 5:18-21).

The great news is that all five of these mentalities have an opposing mentality that pleases God and achieves His purposes. As a person who wants to prevent relapse, you want to learn to think biblically so that you are less prone to turn to any "addiction." In other words, transformed thinking enables you to know God, know what pleases Him, and to live a life that will be of great benefit to you and to God's Kingdom.

As transforming Christians, everything hinges upon our thinking and mind renewal. In fact, as transforming Christians, we are all called to think, speak, and act in the following five new replacement "mentalities": be humble, be giving, be responsible, be grateful, and be submissive. Each of these is the opposite of one of the five detrimental mentalities mentioned first. Here is a diagram to help you:

Put-off	Put-on (Be Transformed)
Entitlement Mentality	Be Humble
Consumer Mentality	Be Giving
Victim Mentality	Be Responsible
Perishing Mentality	Be Grateful
Rebellious Mentality	Be Submissive

The Entitlement Mentality vs. Being Humble

The "entitlement" mentality is at odds with what is commonly called The Great Commandment. In Matthew 22:37-38 Jesus said: **"You shall love the Lord your God with all your heart and with all your soul and with all your mind. This is the great and first commandment."** Basically, any type of "addiction" may manifest when we do not love the Lord God with all of our heart, soul, and *mind*. In other words, a person in active addiction is primarily concerned with pleasing self and not the Lord; all of his faculties (heart, soul, and mind) are consumed with self. There is no loving relationship with the Lord when we are only involved in loving self. It is a one-person relationship that omits God and others. This is true for any and all types of addiction.

Now, the "entitlement" mentality is simply the opposite of obeying the words of Christ in Matthew 22:37-38 above. It is characterized by thinking that we have *rights* to things that are really gifts or privileges given by God. A person in this type of mindset thinks he deserves more than what he is getting. "I deserve better" and "I deserved that but I did not get it" are often what a person in this mode of thinking says to himself. The "addict" who has this mentality wrongly thinks that the things of this earth exist to satisfy and please him! It is a self-centered way of thinking rather than a Christ-centered way of thinking. We must remind ourselves that the earth and all that is in it belong to the Lord; therefore, we are to serve the Lord who is the King of Kings.

The "entitlement mentality is a _____-_____ way of thinking instead of a _____-_____ way of thinking.

How have you manifested the entitlement mentality in the past? Circle the examples below that apply to you and add your own in the space provided:

- I am the center of the universe.
- I should receive every whim and desire I have.
- The world I live in exists for my pleasure.
- I see the privileges God has given to me as "rights."
- I want to prevent all negative consequences from occurring in my life.
- My self-worth and identity come from the things of this world (job, possessions, accomplishments) rather than from a relationship with Christ.

- _____
- _____
- _____

How can you begin living in humility in the future? Circle the examples below that apply to you and add your own in the space provided:

- I am not the center of the universe but an important part of God's plan in this world.

"Those who travel the high road of humility are not troubled by heavy traffic." Alan K. Simpson

- I should accept "no" when I do not receive every whim and desire I have and be thankful regardless.
- The world I live in exists for God's glory not my pleasure.
- I see the privileges God has given to me as undeserved blessings.
- Although I do not want negative consequences and situations in my life, I will accept them as God's will for my life.
- My self-worth and identity come from my relationship with Christ in whom I abide. He is well-pleased with me because of the righteousness of His Son. I now wear His righteousness like a robe!
- I should not think more highly of myself than I do of others (Philippians 2:3-4, Romans 12:3).

- _____
- _____
- _____

In his excellent booklet on humility, Dr. Stuart Scott lists twenty-four manifestations of humility. Dr. Scott uses the Scriptures to tell us what humility looks like in our lives. Some of them are listed here:

- Recognizing and trusting God's character (Psalm 119:66)
- Seeing yourself as having no right to question or judge an Almighty and Perfect God (Psalm 145:17; Romans 9:19-23)
- Focusing on Christ (Philippians 1:21; Hebrews 12:1-2)
- Biblical praying and a great deal of it (1 Thessalonians 5:17; 1 Timothy 2:1-2)
- Being overwhelmed with God's undeserved grace and goodness (Psalm 116:12-19)
- Being thankful and grateful in general toward others (1 Thessalonians 5:18)
- Being gentle and patient (Colossians 3:12-14)
- Seeing yourself as no better than others (Romans 12:16; Ephesians 3:8)
- Having an accurate view of your gifts and abilities (Romans 12:3)
- Being a good listener (James 1:19; Philippians 2:3-4)[18]

The replacement mentality for "entitlement" thinking is to be _____.

What are some specific ways that you can work on possessing a humble mindset this week? (Hint: use Dr. Scott's material listed above.)

"…give thanks in all circumstances; for this is the will of God in Christ Jesus for you" (1 Thessalonians 5:18).

---

[18] Scott, Stuart. (2002) *From Pride to Humility*, Focus Publishing, Bemidji, MN, p. 18-19.

The Consumer Mentality vs. Being Giving

A second mentality that people in active addiction demonstrate is what I call a "consumer" mentality. Similar to the entitlement mentality in several ways, a consumer is someone who "destroys, spends wastefully, squanders, and uses up" things.[19] To consume a product is to use it fully. A fire that consumes a house burns it down to the ground completely. An addict who is a consumer uses everything to its fullest extent, including people!

Those who possess a consumer mentality do not think with a grateful heart. Their desire is to spend all of their possessions upon their own selfish pursuits rather than to help others. This consumer mentality is based upon a failure to follow the second part of the Great Commandment in Matthew 22:39: **"And a second is like it: You shall love your neighbor as yourself."** A "neighbor" in this verse means "near one." Sometimes when we read that verse we think of a next door neighbor who lives beside you. However, a "neighbor" is best understood to be a "near one" meaning someone who is near you in your everyday life. Examples of near ones include family members, colleagues at work, other students at school, friends, and people you see at the grocery store regularly.

So, how should you love your near ones? One way is by giving of your time, talents, and treasures to help someone in need. Being a blessing to others is a crucial component of the committed Christian walk. However, the consumer is primarily concerned with pleasing one person: self. Therefore, his time, talents, and treasures are wrongly spent for selfish pursuits without consideration of others. For example, money may be spent on an "addictive" shopping spree for enjoyment rather than on the electric bill.[20]

A biblical example of a consumer is the prodigal son in Luke 15:11-32. This young man squandered his future inheritance upon luxurious living and ended up in poverty. How have you been a consumer in your past? Circle examples below:

- I found satisfaction in *temporal* things of this world rather than *eternal* things.
- I wanted to give myself everything in abundance so that I would never go "without."
- I wanted comfort at all costs.
- I was too focused upon the pleasures of this world.
- My goals were focused upon temporal achievements rather than heavenward goals. For example, I focused upon seeking pleasure and avoiding all types of pain.

People with a "consumer" mentality do not think with a _____ heart.

---

[19] Merriam-Webster, I. (1996, c1993). *Merriam-Webster's Collegiate Dictionary.* Includes index. (10th ed.). Springfield, Mass., U.S.A.: Merriam-Webster.

[20] Please understand the word "addictive" to describe a shopping spree is a worldly idea and the Bible would describe it as being a poor steward of God-given resources, or idolatry.

Addicts are "takers" and "consumers" and do not demonstrate a _____ heart.

- I alleviated all pain medicinally and with comfort foods (or other temporary pleasures) so that I never had to experience any pain whatsoever in a fallen, sin-cursed, and selfish world.
- I depended upon temporary pleasures rather than upon God to alleviate pain.
- _____
- _____
- _____

Consumers are "takers" and not "givers." Takers are never satisfied with what they consume and they want more and more and more. The world is not designed to satisfy a human being. Only God satisfies completely. Addicts are "takers" and "consumers." They have little thought of giving to others as most of their thoughts revolve around what they can get. This mentality demonstrates an ungrateful heart that will never be content because the heart can never be satisfied with temporary pleasures. The last of the Ten Commandments is against covetousness, which is the opposite of contentment with the things we have. We must remember always that only eternal treasures are satisfying.

The replacement for consumers is to have a _____ _____.

God even calls us to go a step beyond contentment! Rather than thinking like a consumer, Christians must become givers in order to prevent relapse. View yourself not as an owner but as a responsible *steward* who belongs to Christ along with everything you have been given. God owns you and everything He has given to you. You must learn to be giving with what He has given to you. The replacement mentality for consumers is to have a giving heart. The very heart of God is to give to others.

As Christians, we must learn to give to others as though we are giving to God Himself. James 2:15-17 states: **"If a brother or sister is poorly clothed and lacking in daily food, and one of you says to them, 'Go in peace, be warmed and filled,' without giving them the things needed for the body, what good is that? So also faith by itself, if it does not have works, is dead."** Giving demonstrates our faith in Christ and the love of God to others who desperately need to know Him as their loving Creator!

How can you be a giver in the future? Circle examples below:

- I will seek to find satisfaction in *eternal* rather than *temporal* things of this world.
- I will be sensitive to the needs of others and give to them.
- I will not seek personal comforts primarily but will seek to comfort others.
- I will be focused more upon sharing my faith, encouraging others, helping hurting souls, and other eternal pursuits rather than upon the pleasures of this world.
- My goals will be focused upon eternal relationships and helping others rather than temporal achievements that the world encourages.

"... remember the words of the Lord Jesus, how he himself said, 'It is more blessed to give than to receive'" (Acts 20:35b).

- I will not seek to alleviate all of the pain in my life through temporary pleasures (like medicine, food, spending money, etc.). Instead, I will overcome that pain through giving praise to God and helping others.
- I will depend upon God and trust Him to alleviate pain in His perfect timing.
- _____
- _____
- _____

One final note is that you cannot allow your emotions to lead you. Those living in an entitled or consumer mentality live by emotions rather than the commands of God. You must learn to be responsible by doing the right thing no matter how you feel. Obedience does not depend on feelings! In fact, emotions lead us away from obeying God. Make decisions that are right according to God's Word rather than according to your emotional state. Emotional decisions made out of hurt, anger, and fear likely lead to harder consequences rather than life-giving solutions.

The Victim Mentality vs. Being Responsible

The final three mentalities are "victim," "perishing," and "rebellious" thinking, and each manifests in this particular order as described in Ephesians 5:18-21: **"And do not get drunk with wine, for that is debauchery, but be filled with the Spirit, addressing one another in psalms and hymns and spiritual songs, singing and making melody to the Lord with all your heart, giving thanks always and for everything to God the Father in the name of our Lord Jesus Christ, submitting to one another out of reverence for Christ."**

People with a "victim" mentality believe they have been _____ by another person.

A "victim" mentality is the belief that you have been wronged by another person which then develops into an outlook on life that is self-absorbed. It often involves blame-shifting, or directing the blame for a problem onto someone or something other than the guilty party. Victims often feel powerless. True victims are those who have truly been overpowered and harmed by another person without the ability to stop the event. However, those who shift the blame from themselves, when they are truly to blame for their own choices and actions, are not powerless. When you are wrongly hurt or feel wrongly hurt as a victim, you will often turn to an addictive pleasure to feel good in order to escape, cope, and deal with the pain. This choice for an addictive pleasure is not God's best for you and will lead to further problems. When an addict in active addiction trusts only himself, then he feels like he has been wronged by God when his addiction lands him in trouble. Addiction can be this blinding to the truth.

"But put on the Lord Jesus Christ, and make no provision for the flesh, to gratify its desires" (Romans 13:14).

No matter how the victim mentality develops, it often leads to an addictive outlook toward life. You must not allow yourself to develop a victim mentality of feeling like a powerless person who is being taken advantage of unfairly. For example, in Genesis 3:12, Adam blamed his

The replacement for a "victim" mentality is to be _____.

"So then each of us will give an account of himself to God" (Romans 14:12).

"Put to death therefore what is earthly in you: sexual immorality, impurity, passion, evil desire, and covetousness, which is idolatry" (Colossians 3:5).

Father God for his sin and the Lord had done nothing to provoke Adam to sin: **"The man said, 'The woman whom you gave to be with me, she gave me fruit of the tree, and I ate.'"** Notice the language here is "the woman whom you gave to be with me" and implies some culpability on God's part for Adam's sin. The Lord God had done nothing wrong, yet Adam was shifting some of the blame to God and placing partial responsibility upon Him for Adam's sin. Every person I know struggles at times with this same tendency to blame God for his problems. Many "victims" are angry with God.

The issue of taking responsibility and being obedient to the Holy Spirit is mentioned first in the passage that addresses drunkenness and "addiction" in Ephesians 5:18-21 (v.18 only): **"And do not get drunk with wine, for that is debauchery, but be filled with the Spirit…"** There is no way around it: a Spirit-filled life is one in which the person makes righteous decisions that please the Lord. Being responsible and obedient to the Holy Spirit is the very first command to counter drunkenness. A drunkard is irresponsible. A drunkard is disobedient to God. A drunkard is not under the power of the Holy Spirit but under the power of his own flesh. Therefore, he is filled with his flesh and not the Spirit, whereby he fulfills the desires of his flesh and not the desires of God.

From this verse in Ephesians 5:18 is derived the antidote for drunkenness, which is the "filling of the Holy Spirit." This always leads to making responsible choices and obedience to Christ. This is the first requirement that God places upon any transforming addict from any type of addiction: responsibility—rather than being drunk with wine and out of control.

The sinful failures of the addict to be responsible are compounded by wrong thinking—the victim mentality. Here is a typical cycle:

- An addict fails to be responsible.
- A friend or loved one picks up his responsibility and relieves the consequence.
- The addict feels guilty about the sinful failure but experiences no negative consequence.
- The sin causes consequential emotions such as guilt, fear, or anger.
- He mistakenly begins to believe that he is not responsible and that the friend or loved one who picked up the responsibility is actually responsible.
- The addict then becomes resentful of that friend or loved one, sometimes without realizing it.

It is incredible to see how many addicts are bitter and resentful toward the friend or loved one who is simply trying to do the right thing for them. The addict's irresponsibility is covered up superficially, but the guilt associated with the consequences of sin stand as a barrier between the addict and God. This guilt from making sinful choices only goes away by the blood of the Lamb, or the sacrifice of the Lord Jesus Christ. Otherwise, the addict remains truly guilty before God.

How have you blame-shifted in the past and thereby thought like a victim? Circle examples below that apply to you and write in your own in the space provided:

> *"Let no one say when he is tempted, 'I am being tempted by God,' for God cannot be tempted with evil, and he himself tempts no one" (James 1:13).*

- I blamed God for my poor choices.
- I mistakenly thought that I was not required to work, do chores, follow rules, be disciplined, be structured, follow expectations, and experience any negative consequences.
- I excused all my bad choices by blaming other people.
- I blamed my "disease" of addiction rather than myself for poor choices.
- I blamed my environment for my wrong choices.
- I blamed my genetic makeup and my physical body for choices I willingly made.
- I blamed Satan for my choices when he only tempted me.
- I blamed myself for other people's wrong choices when it was clearly their responsibility and fault. I take on too much responsibility for others and allow them to blame me.
- I never talk about my sin, nor do I blame myself for anything.
- I talk about grace but never mention my sin and my very real need for a Savior.
- I do not think about the Gospel as God's forgiveness of my sin so I do not think about my sins or my need to confess and repent of my sins.
- I do not pray or call out to God for forgiveness.
- I do not read the Bible and instead spend hours of time on recreational pursuits (like internet, hobbies, sports, etc.).
- _____
- _____
- _____

The opposite of being a victim is taking responsibility and being obedient to God's Word. Responsibility is the key to experiencing the forgiveness of God and His power to prevent a relapse. God holds all of us responsible for our thoughts, words, and actions. The world's system, in our society, is often too quick to excuse a person's lack of responsibility by blaming it on a so-called disease or his environment or upbringing. "Addiction" is now predominantly viewed as an illness or a disease rather than a sinful thought problem that becomes physically enslaving. At some point along the way, the "addict" is responsible for his or her thoughts and actions that *led to* the "addiction."

The opposite of being a victim is taking _____ and being _____ to God's Word.

How can you learn to be responsible in the future? Circle statements below that you agree with and will implement into your life in the future:

- I will blame myself and not God for my poor choices.

- I know I am required to work, do chores, follow rules, be disciplined, be structured, follow expectations, and sometimes experience negative consequences due to wrong choices.
- I will not excuse all my bad choices by blaming other people.
- I will blame myself (not a man-made "disease" of addiction) for poor choices.
- I will not ignore the impact of my environment that shaped my thinking; however, I will not blame my environment for the wrong choices I made.
- I will not blame my genetic makeup or my physical body for choices I willingly made.
- I will not blame Satan for my choices when he only tempted me.
- I will not blame myself for other people's wrong choices when it was clearly their responsibility and fault. I will not take on too much responsibility for others and allow them to blame me.
- I will be open and talk about my sin, not blaming anything else or anyone else but myself.
- I will talk about grace from God, my sin, and my very real need for a Savior.
- I will think about the Gospel as God's forgiveness of my sin. I will confess my sins and repent of them.
- I will pray and call out to God for forgiveness.
- I will read the Bible instead of spending hours on recreational pursuits (like internet, hobbies, sports, etc.)
- _____
- _____
- _____

One final warning about responsibility is that people who are prone to relapse tend to accept too much responsibility or too little responsibility. Look at your priorities in your life right now. List your priorities in the space provided below and place the most important ones from top to bottom: (examples might be care for spouse, love children, serve in my church, my job, etc.)

What responsibilities have you taken on that are not your concern?

What responsibilities have you denied that should be your concern?

Ask your TCF (Trusted Christian Friend) or a biblical counselor to go over this priority list with you and to help you better prioritize it biblically. Then, work out an action plan for how to address each priority specifically. Use daily, weekly, and monthly goals in the space provided below:

The Perishing Mentality vs. Being Grateful

The next mentality is called a "perishing mentality." This fourth mindset is opposite what is portrayed in the following verses of Ephesians 5:19-20: **"... addressing one another in psalms and hymns and spiritual songs, singing and making melody to the Lord with all your heart, giving thanks always and for everything to God the Father in the name of our Lord Jesus Christ ..."** A perishing mentality is defined as a "woe is me" attitude. It is an extreme manner of thinking that anything that can go wrong will go wrong, with the self-absorbed and defeated mindset that "bad things always happen to me." It is not reflective of a thankful heart. The character, Eeyore, from Winnie the Pooh characterizes the perishing mindset.

Proverbs 31:6-7 describes a perishing mentality: **"Give strong drink to the one who is perishing, and wine to those in bitter distress; let them drink and forget their poverty and remember their misery no more."** Someone who is physically dying due to some type of illness is given strong medications (drink) to allow him to forget his condition. This person is likely in agonizing pain and needs relief. In these cases, the Bible gives the directive to use strong wine (which is a drug in liquid form) to assist this person. God is very gracious by giving us these verses to direct our thinking about physical pain and suffering.

A "perishing" mentality is self-_____ and has a _____ mindset.

It is a _____ way to think.

However, the addict may suffer from emotional pain and may develop a perishing mentality even when there is no physical pain.[21] The Bible refers to the truth that a "crushed spirit" (or a spirit wounded from emotional hurts) is more difficult to bear than physical pain, in Proverbs 18:14: **"A man's spirit will endure sickness, but a crushed spirit who can bear?"** Emotional hurts can overwhelm any of us. It is for this reason that self-

---

[21] Some people get hooked on prescription pain killers that they had been taking for physical pain, but have now found non-physical reasons for taking more medicine. God looks at the heart and the motives for taking the medications.

help groups truthfully say that the "number one offender" for a drunkard is resentment. Resentments develop when we re-live in our minds an experience or perceived hurt in the past or present. It is like ripping the scab off of a wound that is healing—the pain comes back when that wound is re-opened. This reinjuring of the healing wound brings bitterness as one is resenting and re-feeling all the wounds of the past.

You must realize the importance of determining to be like Jesus Christ who had a forgiving spirit toward those who hurt Him. You may not believe that you are able to personally forgive the other person, but if you focus your thoughts on Christ you will develop an attitude of forgiveness. Your pain pales in comparison to the pain Jesus experienced in His earthly life and on the cross. He forgave us and we are among the sinners who are responsible for putting Him on the cross.

The perishing mentality is a destructive way to think. This mindset develops in two ways. When a person focuses upon past hurts so much that they become the center of his universe, the perishing mentality develops quickly. Bringing glory to Jesus Christ must be our main focus and not unforgiven hurts from the past. That is a wrong response to being wronged! 1 Thessalonians 5:15 states: **"See that no one repays anyone evil for evil, but always seek to do good to one another and to everyone."**

"I will sing unto the LORD because He has dealt bountifully with me" (Psalm 13:6).

A perishing mentality may also develop when a person focuses upon what he does not have rather than on what he does possess eternally in Christ. It is a sinful, ungrateful way to think, especially when one has been given eternal life through the forgiveness of Christ. The perishing mentality is mired in self-pity. Self-pity is prideful because it involves too much focus upon yourself and what you are not getting. It is based upon "I am not getting what I deserve and I deserve a whole lot better than this!" The truth is that God is very gracious to us since we all deserve eternal punishment in hell for our sins; but because of Jesus, we are forgiven and spared from what we really deserve.

Those enslaved to addiction have a warped view of what they think they deserve.[22] They do not understand that God's grace has been extended to them in every area of their lives. This way of thinking not only stems from but also breeds more deep resentments which often feed "addictive" behavior. To prevent relapse, you must foster the following biblical concept in your mind: "I deserve worse than what I am getting and I am thankful for God's grace and mercy." Both mercy and grace are unmerited and unearned. One receives these gifts from God through the sacrifice of the Lord Jesus Christ.

---

[22] Here is the connection between an entitlement, a consumer, and a perishing mentality. All of these mindsets breed resentment.

We need to repent of our ungrateful attitudes and turn to God. Repentance from sin is a gift from God (2 Timothy 2:25). It is the kindness and patience of God that should lead us to repentance, according to Romans 2:4: **"Or do you presume on the riches of his kindness and forbearance and patience, not knowing that God's kindness is meant to lead you to repentance?"** Repentance is living God's way in obedience to Him and fills us with all kinds of spiritual blessings. Ask God to grant you the gift of repentance.[23]

How have you manifested the perishing mentality in the past? Circle below some of the examples of statements you may have said in the past and add your own in the space provided:

- "Why do all the bad things happen to me?"
- "Why is God punishing me?"
- "Why can't I have more money (or material possessions)?"
- "My car is nice, but yours is nicer." (discontentment and covetousness)
- "Woe is me!" or "I'm doomed."
- "I wish I could die!"
- "I hate myself."
- "Why aren't my prayers being answered?"
- "Why do I have to be addicted?" (which is also the victim mentality because it is a failure to take responsibility—the word "addict" should be replaced with "sinner" or "idolater" which places the responsibility upon the person).
- "Why doesn't God deliver me from my sinful addiction?"
- _____
- _____
- _____

Note all of the "why" questions above. "Why" questions should rarely, if ever, be asked of God because they tend to question His goodness, love, and sovereignty. Do not "shake your fist" at God and ask "why" questions. Only ask Him *what* He wants to teach you through the trials of your life. James 1:2-3 states: **"Count it all joy, my brothers, when you meet trials of various kinds, for you know that the testing of your faith produces steadfastness."** Here again in these verses, you see the importance of having a joyful mentality based upon the loving character of God and not upon your circumstances. If you want to ask a "why" question to our gracious Father in heaven, then you might ask, "Why are you allowing me to live, Lord, knowing all of the sinful thoughts and choices I made yesterday and in my past?"

Friends and loved ones unwittingly encourage the perishing mentality in those who struggle with addictions. Circle below statements that you have heard OTHERS say in regard to you:

If you have an ungrateful heart, you need to _____ and turn to _____.

"Count it all _____, my brothers, when you meet _____ of various kinds, for you know that the _____ of your faith produces _____" (James 1:2-3).

---

[23] For some reason, some Christians think of repentance as a bad thing and nothing could be further from the truth.

An addict is an idolater interested in pleasing only _____, _____, and _____.

- "I know you have it harder than others."
- "School was harder for you than it was for your brother." Comparisons with others breed the perishing mentality. Always compare yourself with yourself in the past and not with other people. All circumstances are not created equal.
- "We can't do that because we don't have the money. God will have to provide better for us in the future."
- "We aren't as blessed as other people."
- "You just are not as smart as your sister."
- "You are stupid and will never amount to anything."
- "You are not talented."
- _____
- _____
- _____

If you have relapsed, you are probably thinking in this perishing mentality. It is a self-centered focus that shrinks your world down to one person—you. An "addict" and idolater is concerned about pleasing only one person: Me, Myself, and I. That "one person world" is a lonely place to be because few people want to join a world where you are the king! Relationships are always "give and take" and the self-centered person with a perishing mentality will have very few real friendships. In fact, Hebrews 12:15b compares bitterness and resentment to a root that grows, spreads, and defiles many people: **"that no 'root of bitterness' springs up and causes trouble, and by it many become defiled."** Those caught in the trap of active addiction think they have many friends but that is only while they are supplying and participating in the addictive festivities.

A joyful mentality is what replaces the perishing mentality. Ephesians 4:32 reminds us to treat others as we have been treated by the Lord: **"Be kind to one another, tenderhearted, forgiving one another, as God in Christ forgave you."** Joy is a fruit of the Spirit but it is not the same as happiness. Happiness only occurs when my circumstances are good. The word "happy" is derived from the word "happenstance" so that when good circumstances are in place, I am happy. However, when bad circumstances occur, then I am sad. Joy is produced whether my circumstances are good or bad. Joy is the replacement for the perishing mentality.

God is more concerned about your holiness than He is with your happiness. In other words, focus upon learning to be Christ-like by having the correct, biblical mindset that will set you apart from the lies and patterned thinking of this world (Romans 12:2). Then, when you learn to do what God requires—right thinking—the Holy Spirit will produce a joyful mentality inside of you, and you will become "holy," which means "set apart." Isaiah 55:8-9 reminds us of God's holiness and how different He is from us now because of our sinful nature: **"For my thoughts are not your thoughts, neither are your ways my ways, declares the LORD. For as the**

"The thoughts of God's faithfulness must make us confide in Him; the thoughts of God's holiness must make us conform to Him."
Thomas Watson

"We judge men by their actions. God judges men by their thoughts." Thomas Watson

heavens are higher than the earth, so are my ways higher than your ways and my thoughts than your thoughts."

The goal is to think and act like Jesus. In time, you will trust God more, be more stable emotionally, and experience the joy of living a holy life. Holiness is the primary goal and it often produces the fruit of true joy that comes from the Holy Spirit. Do not allow yourself to be ungrateful or to have a perishing mentality. Point yourself to the goodness of God in all things in order to foster a grateful heart. Always pray with a thankful heart.

In the future, how can you learn to be more grateful? Circle the statements below that you will use to help you to apply thankfulness to your own heart:

- I will look for mature Christians who model gratefulness before me.
- I will try to model gratefulness before others.
- I will always point out the good (or grace of God) in any situation that may appear to be bad at first.
- I will find something to be thankful for, even for things that are not desired.
- I will view my circumstances as permitted by God in order to change my character, thereby making me more like Jesus Christ.
- I will not focus on my lack of worldly possessions (i.e. money, opportunity, employment or education). Instead, I will focus upon my eternal possessions: Christ, heaven, and being forgiven.
- I will not be mired in self-pity, or focus too much upon myself in any way.
- I will focus my thoughts upon Christ and have a joyful mentality.
- _____
- _____
- _____

"We cannot ask in behalf of Christ what Christ would not ask himself if He were praying."
A.B. Simpson

The Rebellious Mentality vs. Being Submissive

The "rebellious mentality" of the relapsing person is the fifth and final mentality of addictive thinking. The replacement for this mentality is a submissive spirit. Someone who is rebellious toward the Lord and human authorities acts independently and thinks he is self-sufficient. Only God is self-sufficient and all human beings are dependent upon the Lord and others for help.

Human beings are fallen creatures who are born needy, dependent, insufficient, and weak. For a Christian, these four adjectives should not be offensive but must be embraced because a committed follower of Christ needs the Lord, is dependent upon the Lord and others, is sufficient only in Christ, and relies upon the strength of the Holy Spirit. Self-sufficiency is not the goal for Christians because God wants His children to recognize that each one is dependent upon each other the body of Christ, with Christ as the head of that body.

The replacement for the rebellious mentality is to have a _____ spirit.

71

Think about a person who has a neuromuscular disease. The head no longer controls the hand and other parts of the body. The body of Christ often acts like it has muscular dystrophy or Parkinson's disease but this must not be so! The body of Christ must submit its "limbs" to Christ and not act independently of the Head. True Christ followers are submitted to Christ and to human authorities. True Christ followers are surrendered to Christ, and they value the principle of submission along with the protection and love He provides in earthly authorities which are good.

Many addicts are rebellious and not submissive. They are out of control simply because they are their own final authority. They often act out of emotion. They act as though they are God and God Himself does not exist. There is no fear of the Lord. Proverbs 1:7 reminds us that **"the fear of the Lord is the beginning of knowledge; fools despise wisdom and instruction."** Addicts act in accordance with this biblical truth in that they do not fear the Lord and do not act wisely. Psalm 14:1 states: **"The fool says in his heart, 'There is no God.' They are corrupt, they do abominable deeds, there is none who does good."** Sadly, those with addictive mentalities are acting like a "fools," biblically speaking.

What is a "fool" according to the Bible? A fool is a rebel at heart. There are many, many proverbs about the fool and rebellion is the underlying theme in nearly all of them. Fools are not dumb. In fact, many fools are brilliant people in an intellectual sense. When you think of a fool, you might think of someone who is stupid or ignorant, but that is not what a biblical fool is. A biblical fool is someone who lives as if he is his own god. Fools act independently of God and are not submissive to any human authorities.

Fools get fired from jobs because of their unwillingness to do things according to their employer's rules, not because they are incompetent. Fools wreak havoc in the church because of their lack of submission to God's Word and the pastors who care for them. Fools end up alone or with very few friends because they are self-centered and selfish.

"Like a dog that returns to his vomit is a fool who repeats his folly" (Proverbs 26:11).

Unfortunately, addicts are often fools at heart. People actively in an addiction of any type are rebels at heart. They say things to themselves like, "I answer to no one. I do what I want when I want. My will be done." The rebellious mentality pervades their decision-making and sense of justice. Right and wrong decisions are based upon their own sense of justice and not upon God's Word. It is a self-centered way of thinking that revolves around the addict. No one else can live in harmony with a person who thinks this way because the standard is not God's absolute standard from the Scriptures but depends upon the whim of the addict. There is absolutely no pleasing or pacifying a foolish, rebellious heart, even in a three year old child!

Consider how the previous mentalities have led to this final rebellious stage. First, you have a person who thinks he is entitled to have everything he wants in this life. "It's my right," he mistakenly thinks. Second, this person consumes everything he gets in life on himself for selfish pleasure. Third, he becomes frustrated when he fails to get what he wants and he either blames others, including God, or he believes it is entirely his fault. Both of these extremes of thinking are self-absorbed and lead him to believe he is a powerless victim. Feeling powerless, angry, hurt, bitter, and fearful, this person now has a perishing outlook toward life that "anything that can go wrong will go wrong and usually does go wrong for me." His focus remains upon himself and he becomes mired in self-pity.

At this rebellious stage of this person's life, who do you think he trusts the most? The answer is himself. Even if he thinks everything is completely his fault, he wrongly concludes that he must be the one to pull himself out of the situation. He trusts in himself, not God. If he thinks others have brought him to this stage, he then will become more angry and bitter and will certainly not turn to anyone else for help since no one else can be trusted. At this point, he may not be completely broken, but he will simply rely upon himself and no one else. He will relapse again—it is just a matter of time. Officially, this person is called a rebel and a "fool," biblically speaking.

A person with a perishing mentality focuses upon himself and becomes mired in _____-_____.

How have you acted like a rebel? Circle some of the statements that apply to you and add your own in the blank space provided:

- I have learned to be self-reliant.
- I cannot count on anyone but myself.
- I value independence and never want to ask for help.
- I do not trust God to have my best interests at heart.
- I demand that my schedule be adhered to by my family and friends. I will not yield my schedule of things I want and need to do very often.
- My home is not Christ-centered but centered on other things.
- I put myself ahead of my spouse and children in a selfish manner.
- I am a "know-it-all."
- I do not listen to others.
- I do not listen to advice.
- I do not believe others want to help me without some "strings attached."
- I do not respect others.
- Most people I know do not deserve respect.
- I disrespect older people.
- I disrespect younger people.
- I want to control everything in my environment.
- I must make all the decisions in my life.
- I will not ask for another person's help because I value self-sufficiency.
- I do not go to church.
- I have high self-esteem since my hard work is the primary reason for all of my successes in life rather than the Lord.

"I hold back my feet from every evil way, in order to keep your word" (Psalm 119:101).

- I seek to glorify myself.
- I want the glory and importance of positions and power rather than humbly submitting to Christ.
- I do not really believe that a higher being exists that is totally in charge of all things. In other words, God is alive but He is not actively involved in my life.
- I do not believe there is a God.
- I make other people the center of my universe and not Christ.
- I would do anything for my addictive pleasure.
- I live for myself and my own pleasures.
- I can do whatever I want to do.
- I can do whatever I want when I want to do it.
- I do not have to obey my employer (or other authorities like parents or teachers).
- I do not have to follow the rules.
- I am an exception to the rules.
- Even though my authorities tell me not to, I do what I think is best anyway.
- _____
- _____
- _____

"Teach me to do your will, for you are my God" (Psalm 143:10a).

A foreign concept for many people today is the idea of "submission." We are to submit our individual wills to God's. He is our ultimate authority. In all areas of life, God places human beings in places of authority over us to whom we are to submit. This authority begins in the home with the parents who are to enforce God's rules using the rod and reproof. The authority continues at the workplace where a boss is in authority over employees and has the power to discipline and to terminate their job. God has also placed the government as an authority over mankind with the power of "the sword" (so it says in the Bible, meaning punishment for law-breakers) to enforce God's laws. Finally, the church has God-given authority with the power to exercise church discipline for the purpose of calling a sinning believer to repentance and right relationship with Christ.

God commands us to submit to Him in the First Commandment: **"You shall have no other gods before Me"** (Exodus 20:3). Then, authority is emphasized on a human level as it begins in the home according to the Fifth Commandment: **"Honor your father and mother ..."** (Exodus 20:12). Submission is an essential concept for the betterment of society and the betterment of a human being. People who fail to submit end up injured in the hospital, imprisoned in jail, or dead in the grave. If you never learned submission as a child, learn it now, before it's too late!

Being submissive and servant-minded is the key to overcoming a rebellious mentality. Jesus, who is God, had the right to be king, yet He came to serve us. He did not come to be served and He gave His life as a ransom for the salvation of many, according to Matthew 20:25-28: **"But**

Jesus called them to him and said, "You know that the rulers of the Gentiles lord it over them, and their great ones exercise authority over them. It shall not be so among you. But whoever would be great among you must be your servant, and whoever would be first among you must be your slave, even as the Son of Man came not to be served but to serve, and to give his life as a ransom for many." Rebels do not serve anyone else unless it profits them. They often do not love unconditionally. Rebels often love with "strings attached." They often do not have a servant's mindset, which was the mind of Christ described in Matthew 20.

Pride is the hindrance to being servant-minded. Pride feeds a rebel's heart. When a home revolves around one person as though he or she is the center of the family's universe, that person will develop rebel-like symptoms that will manifest when he doesn't get his way. That is when you will see temper tantrums occur no matter what the age of a person—even adult-aged children will throw temper tantrums, "guilt trips," and manipulation ploys to get their way.

The key to overcoming a rebellious mentality is being _____ and _____-_____.

A transformed addict who will not relapse has a humble spirit and desires to learn and practice the principle of submission as seen in the last verse of Ephesians 5:18-21: **"And do not get drunk with wine, for that is debauchery, but be filled with the Spirit, addressing one another in psalms and hymns and spiritual songs, singing and making melody to the Lord with all your heart, giving thanks always and for everything to God the Father in the name of our Lord Jesus Christ, submitting to one another out of reverence for Christ."** "Submitting to one another out of reverence for Christ" demonstrates the powerful fruit of humility.

Submission may be simple to understand but it is not easy to do. Why? Because our fleshly habits fight against the Holy Spirit that dwells within us. Romans 7:21-25 explains this internal war: **"So I find it to be a law that when I want to do right, evil lies close at hand. For I delight in the law of God, in my inner being, but I see in my members another law waging war against the law of my mind and making me captive to the law of sin that dwells in my members. Wretched man that I am! Who will deliver me from this body of death? Thanks be to God through Jesus Christ our Lord! So then, I myself serve the law of God with my mind, but with my flesh I serve the law of sin."**

"Everyone that is proud in heart is an abomination to the LORD" (Proverbs 16:5a).

In the flesh, we want to be self-reliant, independent, and strong. In the flesh, we want to serve our own desires. "If it feels good, then do it" is a worldly lie that feeds the flesh. The biblical principle of not doing whatever you feel like, but doing what God commands, is essential to having a growing relationship with God, spouse, children, friends, church family members, extended family, and co-workers. We must all learn to say "no" to the flesh and to say "yes" to the Holy Spirit. This is why I teach that a Spirit-filled life takes twice the amount of effort, but it is necessary to prevent relapse. The Lord Jesus illustrated this point well in Matthew 26:39-44.

"Whoever exalts himself will be humbled, and whoever humbles himself will be exalted" (Matthew 23:12).

The worldly lie that feeds the flesh is "_____ _____"

And going a little farther he fell on his face and prayed, saying, "My Father, if it be possible, let this cup pass from me; nevertheless, not as I will, but as you will." And he came to the disciples and found them sleeping. And he said to Peter, "So, could you not watch with me one hour? Watch and pray that you may not enter into temptation. The spirit indeed is willing, but the flesh is weak." Again, for the second time, he went away and prayed, "My Father, if this cannot pass unless I drink it, your will be done." And again he came and found them sleeping, for their eyes were heavy. So, leaving them again, he went away and prayed for the third time, saying the same words again. Then he came to the disciples and said to them, "Sleep and take your rest later on. See, the hour is at hand, and the Son of Man is betrayed into the hands of sinners. Rise, let us be going; see, my betrayer is at hand."

Jesus prayed three times asking the Father to remove the heavy burden of going to the cross and being separated from the Father. That was Jesus' will as a human being. Nevertheless, He submitted to the will of the Father each time. In verse 39, Jesus says, **"Not as I will, but as You will"** and that is the lesson of submission demonstrated by our Lord. Jesus said **"Your will be done"** again in verse 43. What is great about our Lord Jesus as a Man is that not only does He say the right things, as in these two verses, but He does the right things, as evidenced by His obedience in going to the cross. Jesus is not a hypocrite because His words match His actions every time. Jesus is not a liar but is faithful to His Word. You and I are to become like Him by emulating His words and actions. We are to have His attitude of obedience: "Not my will, Lord, but yours."

Submission is the "willful placement of our self under an authority." Submission literally means to "yield our self to the will of another."[24] It can also be called "surrender." Is that not what God calls all followers of Christ to do—surrender? We surrender our will to God and the human authority He has set in place over us as an act of faith in God.

"Let every person be subject to the governing authorities. For there is no authority except from God, and those that exist have been instituted by God" (Romans 13:1).

I like to remind myself daily that God is my Owner. He created me. He redeemed me by the blood of Christ. He purchased me back from Satan. Therefore, He owns me and He is a good Master. It is not like I am submitting to an evil person! I am submitting to the most loving, gracious Person I have ever known, my Lord and Savior. Even so, in my flesh, I want to trust myself more than Christ. How ridiculous is that? I know that my ways always get me into trouble and I know that His ways are life-giving. He is my Good Shepherd according to Psalm 23. I must trust Him and trust His Holy Word because my life is now hidden in Christ (Colossians 3:3).

[24] Merriam-Webster, Inc. *Merriam-Webster's Collegiate Dictionary*. Includes index. 10th ed. Springfield, Mass., U.S.A.: Merriam-Webster, 1996, c1993.

People ask me, "Does God really own me?" To which I respond emphatically, "YES!" 1 Corinthians 6:19-20 states this biblical truth in this manner: **"Or do you not know that your body is a temple of the Holy Spirit within you, whom you have from God? You are not your own, for you were bought with a price. So glorify God in your body."** Through the blood of Christ, you were purchased and redeemed back from Satan. In reality, everyone has an owner. One either belongs to Satan or to God, according to Jesus in John 8:44: **"You are of your father the devil, and your will is to do your father's desires. He was a murderer from the beginning, and has nothing to do with the truth, because there is no truth in him. When he lies, he speaks out of his own character, for he is a liar and the father of lies."**

Right now, you are either owned by Satan, if not yet "born again" (John 3:3), or you are owned by the Lord. You must wrestle with this truth to understand who your owner really is. You may think that you are independent, in charge, and "the boss," but that is only a deception of Satan. Satan wants people to think they are in charge of their lives when he really is. To serve self is to serve Satan. To serve Christ is to serve God who is the rightful Owner of all living creatures.

Submission is the_____ placement of our _____ under an authority.

How can you adopt a submissive mentality in the future? Circle statements below that you will be willing to embrace in your life and add your own:

- I will learn to rely upon God through prayer.
- I will learn to trust in God through daily meditation upon the Bible.
- I will read the Word regularly.
- I will ask a more mature, same-gender person to disciple me and I will do what he/she says to do.
- I will ask others for help.
- I will value inter-dependence and seek to help others while asking for help as needed.
- I will trust God as having my best interests at heart.
- I will not insist upon having others follow my schedule.
- My home will be Christ-centered, not centered on me, others, or other things.
- I will put the needs of my spouse and children ahead of my own.
- I will be teachable and not be a "know-it-all."
- I will listen to others, not seeking always to be heard.
- I will listen to advice.
- I will believe others when they say that they want to help me without some "strings attached."
- I will respect others.
- I will learn that most people I know deserve respect.
- I will respect older people.
- I will respect younger people.

- I will relinquish control of everything in my environment.
- I will ask for wisdom from my pastor, disciple-maker, and TCF before making major decisions in my life.
- I will go to church.
- I will find my self-worth in Christ and credit Him as the primary reason for all of my successes in life.
- I will seek to glorify my Lord and Savior.
- I will value eternal things more than temporal things.
- I will choose to believe that God is totally in charge of all things. In other words, God is alive and He is actively involved in my life.
- I believe there is a God.
- I will not make other people the center of my universe but be sure to elevate Christ to that place in my life (since He is already).
- I will not do anything toward fulfilling an addictive pleasure.
- I will not live for myself and my own pleasures.
- I recognize that I cannot do whatever I want to do.

- I cannot do whatever I want when I want to do it.
- I must obey my employer (or other authorities like parents, teachers, etc.).
- I must follow the rules.
- I am not an exception to the rules.
- When my authorities tell me not to do something, I will obey them—even if I think I have a better idea.

- _____
- _____
- _____

Conclusion

Satan wants to tempt you to be your own boss like he tempted Adam and Eve in Genesis 3:5: **"For God knows that when you eat of it your eyes will be opened, and you will be like God, knowing good and evil."** Satan wants you to believe you can be your own god, not required to answer to anyone. Revelation 20:12 tells us that we will give an account to God in eternity: **"And I saw the dead, great and small, standing before the throne, and books were opened. Then another book was opened, which is the book of life. And the dead were judged by what was written in the books, according to what they had done."**

One day you will stand before the Lord and answer to Him for what you did or did not do with what He gave you. You do not own your possessions or your life! God does, and He expects you to live like the Lord Jesus Christ who laid down His life willingly by experiencing death upon the cross.

Simplify your relapse prevention strategy. Simply work on becoming humble, giving, responsible, grateful and submissive in your spirit. Review

List the 5 mentalities you must adopt to be transformed and prevent relapse:

1.

2.

3.

4.

5.

Matthew 22:37-40 and Ephesians 5:18-21 to help you remember this new way to be human! Do not try to do too much. Rather, focus upon your own thinking, speaking, and actions. If you are concerned that you cannot do this without help, then that is a good place to be! Ask your pastor, a leader in your church, a trusted Christian friend, or a biblical counselor to help you.[25] You need the help of others so do not attempt to prevent relapse or be transformed alone.

Learning these relapse prevention strategies and doing them will provide you with more opportunities to advance the kingdom of heaven by living to glorify our great Father in Heaven who alone is worthy of all praise, glory, and honor. It is a new way to be human: to be Christ-like. Learn about God through an intimate, disciple-making relationship with a same-gender mentor. Learn more about God through your study of the Bible so that you can know Him better and trust Him more with your life. That will be a life not focused on the fear of the next relapse, but focused upon living for a loving King. That new life will be a life worth living now and for all of eternity!

So how do you prevent a relapse? Just say "no"? Is that all there is to it: just saying "no" to drugs and alcohol? Of course not! The real answer is that you must learn to say "yes" to Christ. Saying "yes" to Christ is how the Holy Spirit will transform you as you learn to trust and obey God's Word and all of His commands. In order to prevent a relapse from occurring, you must be transformed by the renewing of your mind (Romans 12:2) which will happen gradually in your life as you obediently practice thinking, speaking, and doing what is right, even in the little things. A person who wants to prevent relapse has integrity, which means doing the right thing when no one is watching. "Practice makes perfect" is a cliché but the truth is that practicing righteousness in thoughts, words, and actions makes one like the perfect Person, Jesus Christ.

God has two goals for you. First, He wants you to glorify Him (1 Corinthians 10:31). In other words, He wants you to make Him look good to a lost and dying world. He wants to be known and He works through you to reveal His true character to a sinful, fallen, polluted, and corrupted world ruined by mankind's sin. Second, God wants to change you and make you more like His Son (Romans 8:29). Most people really do not want to change. They are comfortable where they are, but the Lord wants you to be transformed into a new creation. Adopt His goals and implement them in your life in every way.

My former pastor used to say, "You will never say 'no' until you have a bigger 'yes'." In other words, you will never say 'no' to sin until you say 'yes' to righteousness, or making godly choices. Christians have no excuse because they can say 'yes' to Christ through the power of the Holy Spirit who lives within a believer (2 Timothy 1:14) according to Philippians 2:13:

[25] Go to www.nanc.org to find a list of biblical counselors in your area.

"for it is God who works in you, both to will and to work for His good pleasure." Be encouraged that Christ is sufficient and His Word works in partnership with the Holy Spirit to bring about real, lasting, and eternal change in the hearts of His people. The life of a devoted Christ-follower is exciting, fruitful, and powerful when the Holy Spirit is in charge.

Appendices

Appendix A
The Gospel is "Good News"

If you are reading this section of the book, there is probably some question in your mind as to whether or not you are a Christian.[26] Where you are going to spend eternity should be a big concern to you. Unfortunately, many people believe that there is no afterlife, but that's not what the Bible teaches. The Bible tells us that life on earth is temporary and there is definitely an afterlife. Matthew 25:46 quotes Jesus, who said, **"And these will go away into eternal punishment, but the righteous into eternal life."**

Those who are born again by the Holy Spirit have become Christians and will spend their eternal life with the Heavenly Father. Those who do not become Christians will spend their eternal life in an unspeakably horrible place called Hell. Therefore, everyone will inherit one of these two eternal destinations after life on earth.

To appreciate the fact that the Gospel message is good news, you must first hear the bad news. In the beginning, God created a perfect place with two perfect people: Adam and Eve. These two persons willingly chose to disobey God's Word to them (Genesis 3) and when they did, the consequences of their sin was separation from God and each other. Sin always separates. Now, whenever someone is born, he or she is born in the likeness and image of Adam, according to Genesis 5:3: **"When Adam had lived 130 years, he fathered a son in his own likeness, after his image, and named him Seth."** In other words, all persons are now born with a sinful, selfish nature that will naturally lead them away from the living God unless they are "born again" (John 3:3).

The result of this separation is that apart from Christ you are helpless and sinful. More bad news is that everyone is in spiritual bondage, alienated from God because of sin, and headed for the eternal destination of hell. Knowledge of sin comes by the law of God which is found in His Word of Truth. God, in his justice, punishes sinners. You cannot save yourself in any way from this punishment. God is serious about sin and He will punish sinners who are not saved by grace through their faith in Jesus Christ.

Jesus alone saves you by grace through faith in Him. His blood was shed to atone for your sins. Eternal life with God is a gracious, free gift from Him. Ephesians 2:8-9 puts it this way: **"For by grace you have been saved through faith. And this is not your own doing; it is the gift of God, not a result of works, so that no one may boast."** Therefore, you cannot come to God in your own strength, with your good deeds, and ask for eternal life unless God draws you to Himself.

Jesus suffered and died for sinners. His blood atones for your sins. The Lord calls sinners like you and me to repent, or turn from sin, and to turn to God. You are given a new heart and a new nature so that you do not have to remain a slave to sin. You are saved to joyfully obey and serve the Lord for His own glory and purposes.[27] God's plan and purposes for you may take you in a different direction than you wanted to go, but you can trust His character because He

---

[26] This entire appendix has been excerpted from *The Heart of Addiction* by Mark Shaw, Focus Publishing, Bemidji, MN, 2006.

[27] Kruis, John G. *Quick Scripture Reference for Counseling*, Grand Rapids, MI: Baker Books, p. 6.

is loving and faithful. God loves His people and no longer sees them as unrepentant sinners, but as sons and daughters who have a relationship with Him.

No one starts out this life in neutral, as everyone is born in sin and then commits more sin during life. No sin is too big for you to repent of and for God to forgive. No one can earn the gift of eternal life nor does anyone deserve it. Eternal life is a free gift; you cannot earn it or pay for it. Is there any reason why you would not want to pray to receive Jesus Christ as your personal Savior right now? I encourage you to pray right now.

I always recommend that you pray from your heart to God. Do not be concerned about the words you use. In your prayer, confess your sin to God, admit you are a sinner who has lived independently from Him, that you have not earned or deserve the free gift of eternal life, and that you desire to have an intimate relationship with God, your Creator, now and forevermore.

When you become a Christian, your new heart and its love for God causes you to want to do whatever pleases Him because He deserves it and He saved you from the penalty of your sins. Now, you have the Holy Spirit's power living inside you to please and obey your new Father God. If you are truly trusting in Christ and have truly been "born again," you can, and will seek to, now obey any and all of God's commands by His gracious power that lives inside of you.

One word of caution: do not trust in your own words or in your prayer, but trust in God's Son, His Holy Word, and His power to save you from your sins and grant you repentance, a new life, and eternal salvation.

Appendix B
Your Life Story

Writing your life story has several purposes and many benefits. One purpose for writing a life story is that it serves as a "memorial stone" for you and your children about what great things the Lord has done in your life. After the Israelites crossed over the Jordan River in a miraculous event ordained by God, the Lord commanded them to get large memorial stones to commemorate the event and be a reminder to teach future generations about what God had done in their lives. Joshua 4:6-7 states:

> **... that this may be a sign among you. When your children ask in time to come, "What do those stones mean to you?" then you shall tell them that the waters of the Jordan were cut off before the ark of the covenant of the Lord. When it passed over the Jordan, the waters of the Jordan were cut off. So these stones shall be to the people of Israel a memorial forever.**

Like Israel, how does your personal story fit into the grand story of God's redemption of sinful mankind? This exercise will hopefully help you to see how you fit into God's plan better than you saw it previously.

Before writing your life story, take a large piece of poster board; write out a time line from birth to the present. It will look something like this across your poster board:

Birth_____Present

Now, use pictures and symbols to identify those people, events, and life circumstances that had an impact upon your life: positive or negative. Use symbols to depict the progression of your life's journey. Take 4 to 6 hours to do this one phase of preparing for your life history. You should try to complete this alone, but you may need the help of a close friend or family member to help you fill in the blanks.

After you finish the time line of your life's journey, spend a little time reflecting upon how God used key people, events, and life circumstances for your growth. Now, identify on the poster board the various phases of development in your life. Look at these seasons of growth and identify the period of time and key people involved in your journey. Notice how the time line gives you a big picture perspective and provides new insights and encouragement about God's faithfulness in your life.[28]

Now, write out your life story using the time line you just completed. Write it out as though you are writing a novel and make it as detailed and interesting as you can without embellishing or lying! Take the freedom in Christ to author your own book about your life, but remember to include how you learned life lessons, biblical principles, new insights, and how you see God's sovereign, loving, and guiding Hand. One of the main points of this exercise is for you to create a "memorial stone" to remind you, your children and your grandchildren about the goodness and sovereignty of your Creator and Heavenly Father. Do not leave God out of your life story as He is the most important character!

---

[28] Wailing, Terry, *Focusing Leaders*, CRM, 1998, page 3.5.

Appendix C
Is Addiction *Really* a "Disease?"

A topic of debate I am often involved in is whether or not an addiction is a "disease." I do not have space to address this subject comprehensively here, but let me make just a few points in this appendix to address this debate biblically.

First, the Bible never refers to addiction as a disease but as a sin issue. Some words the Bible does not include: drunkenness, sin, witchcraft, and idolatry.

Second, the idea of addiction as a "disease" is a relatively new idea, less than 80 years old as of this writing. Originally, the terms addiction and "alcoholism" were regarded as being similar to a "disease," as this was only a theory. Now, most people accept the disease concept theory as a fact without much constructive thought!

Finally, the language today surrounding the sin of addiction (even the word "addiction" itself) is very scientific-sounding. Words like recovery, relapse, and disease sound so scientific and medical that most people do not question this new belief in our society. Below is a chart that compares God's Words on addiction with the worldly concepts presented by Satan (note that much of the world's terminology uses good words, but they do not go far enough to point us to the redeeming power of Christ):

GOD'S WORD & HIS CHURCH	SELF-HELP GROUPS
Sin	Disease
Transformation (Romans 12:2)	Recovery
Disciple-maker, Undershepherd or pastoral relationships	Sponsor
Sin	Relapse
Born with a sinful nature	Born basically good with a bad disease or environment
Church attendance and participation	Go to meetings every day if possible
Fellowship with other believers with prayer, biblical principles, encouragement, and truth	Most self-help meetings are called a "fellowship" and often have fun outings to socialize
Bible Studies with other Christians to learn and grow in the wisdom of God	Secular book studies on recovery principles at self-help meetings to grow in the wisdom of mankind
Ask forgiveness—must be for benefit of others and the glory of God before self and to reconcile the relationship according to Luke 17:3-10	Make amends—often a selfish benefit and motive to clear one's own conscience; sometimes take others into consideration but not a primary motivation
Adoption into the family of Christ; you become a "son" or "daughter" of the Most High God	Acceptance into the fellowship of people of all religions; you become a "label" for life identifying you by your sin forever

Promote church attendance	Discourage church attendance; promote self-help
Members are Christian believers and seek to save the lost: unbelievers	Members are "spiritual" people vs. "earth" people who just do not understand the self-help program
Sin nature problem from within; self is problem	Disease from without problem; self is victim
Bible contains many principles to apply to an individual's life with freedom and liberty in Christ	Program is simple with instructions to follow but everyone must work those same principles
Responsibility is key: confess AND hate AND forsake your sin because it displeases God	Responsibility is key, but then blame your "disease"—sends a mixed, confusing message
Confess behaviors and thoughts as sin; Jesus died for sin and sinners, not a lifelong "disease," so the power of addiction has been overcome	State that your behaviors and thoughts are caused by a theoretical disease of addiction that you will cope with the rest of your life never to overcome fully
Gospels tell about the life of Jesus and serves as a model for trying to live more like Him everyday	Secular recovery book gives you examples from others who are now living a sober life
Follow Christ	Follow the program, principles, and people
The Lord Jesus Christ, who chooses me (Ephesians 1)	A "higher power" of one's own choosing

Since the 1930's, the idea that "alcoholism" was like a "disease" was popularized by two men and spread like wildfire, but is it true? Look at the following passages on drunkenness and see what the Lord says about this problem Himself in His Holy Word. Notice the devastating consequences of drunkenness and how it offends our perfect God. While the world glamorizes and minimizes drunkenness, the Bible tells us the honest and severe consequences of such thinking and behaving.

This is by no means a comprehensive list. There are more passages of Scripture on drunkenness. Take the time and find your own scriptures. If you exhaust all of those verses, then research all of the verses related to the topics of idolatry, sorcery, witchcraft, gluttony, lust, adultery, lying, etc. (These are not popular topics because they are brutally honest about the devastation of our sins, but they can serve as reminders for why it is so vital NOT to drink excessively or to abuse drugs.)

What God Says About Drunkenness

Genesis 9:20-23	Genesis 19:30-38	Deuteronomy 21:18-21
1 Samuel 1:14-15	1 Samuel 25:36-37	Proverbs 31:4-7
Isaiah 19:14	Isaiah 24:20	Jeremiah 25:27
Jeremiah 51:7	Habakkuk 2:15	Luke 12:45-46
Isaiah 28:1-4 & verses 7-8	Jeremiah 23:9	Joel 3:3
Hosea 4:10-11	Proverbs 20:1	Proverbs 21:17
Proverbs 23:20-21	Proverbs 23:29-35	Luke 21:34
Ephesians 5:15-21	1 Corinthians 6:9-11	1 Corinthians 5:11
1 Thessalonians 5:7	1 Peter 4:3	Revelation 18:3

Appendix D
Counting the Cost

How devastating have the consequences been from your recent relapse and from addiction in general? Use this worksheet to determine the life-devastating consequences you now must face as a result of your problem of addiction. This is a sobering exercise that may wake you out of denial.

Marital: If you are married, list the ways that your addictive choices have affected your intimacy with your spouse. Be sure to include lying, manipulation, control, poor communication, secrets, sexual problems, finances, in-law problems, and other hindrances to being "one flesh" according to biblical standards.

Economic/Financial: Figure out how much money you spent on your addictive choices in a typical day. Be sure to include gas, hotel rooms, phone bills, paying for others to use drugs, overdrawn bank accounts, and other related expenses.

Homework Assignment:

Now, figure out an estimate of how much you spent on your addictive choices in a typical week by multiplying the amount for one day (above) by the number of days you used in a typical week? For example, some people use 3-4 days a week so they would multiply 4 days by the number for one day reached above. Some used all 7 days so they would multiply it by 7. Now, estimate how much you spent on your addictive choices during the past 12 months. For example, 52 weeks multiplied by thc amount in the weekly estimate above.

Example:

NAME OF EXPENSE	ESTIMATE COST PER 1 DAY	COST PER WEEK (Last column x 7 days usually)	TOTAL YEARLY COST (Last column x 52 weeks)
Buying Alcohol	$5.00	$35.00 ($5 x 7 days)	$1,820.00 ($35 x 52 weeks)
Buying Drugs	$100.00	$300.00 (only used 3 days so $100 x 3 days)	$15,600.00 ($300 x 52 weeks)
Hotel Rooms	$40.00	$80.00 (only used 2 days so $40 x 2 days)	$4,160.00 ($80 x 52 weeks)
Gas/Cell Phone	$5.00	$15.00 (only used 3 days so $5 x 3 days)	$780.00 ($15 x 52 weeks)
Overdrawn Bank	$20.00	$20.00 (1x per month)	$240.00 ($20 x 12 months)
		Yearly Total	$22,600.00

Obviously, this is just an example, but it is staggering to think about how much money is wasted on drugs and alcohol per year.

Consider your addiction in light of the following important areas of your life. Too often we think of it without considering as a personal issue or choice.

Social
- How has your addiction affected your relationships with friends? How has it affected your relationships with church family and friends?
- How close are you to your pastor and church leaders?
- How has your addiction affected your relationships with co-workers?
- How have you treated people in general at the grocery store, gas station, etc.?

Physical
- Rate your health on a scale from 1 to 10 (10 being in great health).
- How has your addiction caused your health to deteriorate? Name the ways.
- If you smoke cigarettes or used to smoke drugs, go to a pulmonary doctor to assess the condition of your lungs.
- What exercise did you give up for your addiction?
- What eating habits did you develop that are not good for your health?
- Do you drink water?
- Did you take care of your personal hygiene when using drugs?

Emotional
- What emotions do you struggle with the most: depression, self-pity, anger, worry, fear, etc.?
- In what ways did your addiction *help* you to manage those emotions?
- In what ways did your addiction *hurt* you in managing those emotions?
- Are you a "feelings-oriented" person who must do what he/she feels?
- Do you give into your feelings too much so that they tend to control you or lead you, rather than you controlling them?

Familial
- In what ways has your addiction affected relationships with family members (parents, siblings, children, extended family, etc.)?
- What things have you done to hurt those relationships (steal, lie, cheat, manipulate, control)?

Occupational
- In what ways have you cheated your employer? Be specific. Examples of cheating your employer include: not getting to work on time, being "hung-over" and not your best at work, and having your mind focused upon craving the drug rather than work.
- Have you stolen from your employer in any other way?

Legal: Whether or not you have gotten caught, how have you broken the law? For example, breaking the law can be as simple as speeding in your vehicle or dealing drugs. Be specific.

Spiritual:
- In what ways has your addiction been more of a priority to you than being obedient to God?

- How much have you attended church this past year?
- Have you been active in your church participation beyond just showing up every Sunday for a worship service?

When was the first time you drank alcohol/used drugs?
- Describe the circumstances around that first time of drinking/drug usage.
- How many years did you drink/use drugs since that first time?
- Have you had periods of sobriety?
- If so, for how long, and under what circumstances were you able to refrain from alcohol and drugs during that time?
- How often did you drink alcohol/use drugs this past week? _____ List number of days
- If you have had a period of sobriety in the past week, then when you were drinking/using drugs regularly, how many days out of the week did you use on average? _____
- What is your drug of choice?
      Second choice?
      Third choice?
- Estimate: How much time did you spend thinking about your drug of choice yesterday?
- How much time have you spent thinking about it already today?
- List the things that you have done in the past, that you now regret, because of your love for drugs and the bad choices you made? (Ask God to forgive you for these things. Keep this list of people you've hurt because you now need to pray and find a way to ask forgiveness of them for your selfishness.)

What have I DONE?	Who was affected by my actions (or inaction)?	Plan for FORGIVENESS:

Appendix E
Dealing with Past Abuse

This topic deserves much more time than I can devote to it here in this appendix, but a common question asked of biblical counselors by those who have struggled with addictions is: "If God is good, why would he let me go through all of the abuse I've gone through?"

This question might be asked by someone who was sexually abused as a child, raped, verbally put down by a spouse, physically beaten by a parent, and so on. Sadly, there are too many abusive scenarios to list them all here.

So the question is, why does a loving, good God allow people to be sinned against and hurt? We know that we must learn how to rebound from two situations in life: (1) sinful choices that we make and (2) sinful choices that others make against us. This workbook primarily deals with the first situation of dealing with our own sinful choices. However, this appendix will briefly deal with the sin of others against us.

In Genesis 3, Adam and Eve sinned against God by deliberately disobeying His command in Genesis 2:15-17: **"The LORD God took the man and put him in the garden of Eden to work it and keep it. And the LORD God commanded the man, saying, "You may surely eat of every tree of the garden, but of the tree of the knowledge of good and evil you shall not eat, for in the day that you eat of it you shall surely die."** God could have stepped in and prevented their sinful choices. God could have caused an earthquake to shake them just before they ate to get their attention before they sinned. God could have intervened in many ways. So why didn't He?

God gave Adam a warning of the consequence that would come if he disobeyed: death. Eve was not yet created since she was brought to life several verses AFTER God spoke to Adam (Genesis 2:21-22). So Adam was responsible for telling Eve God's Word accurately so that they would both obey Him.

Today, God warns us all with His Holy Word. God tells us of the impending consequences of sin. For example, in Ephesians 5:18, God says that a life of drunkenness will lead to debauchery, or utter ruin: **"And do not get drunk with wine, for that is debauchery, but be filled with the Spirit ..."** So whose fault is it when someone gets a DUI for driving under the influence of alcohol? Even if they have not read the Word of God, that person is still responsible before God and will experience the consequences of a ruined, debauched life if they live a drunken lifestyle.

When we consider physical and emotional abuse suffered at the hands of others, we need to remember that the sinful choices of people are despicable to God. God hates sin. Psalms 5 and 7 speak of God's hatred for iniquity and deceit. The indignation, or anger, that God feels every day (Psalm 7:11) is due to the injustices that He sees on this earth and that includes all types of abuse. This world is no longer the perfect world that God designed in Genesis 1 & 2 because of the willful disobedience and sin of mankind in Genesis 3. From Genesis 3 through Revelation 21, the Bible deals with a world that is sinful, fallen, and broken because of man's sins. Only chapters 21 & 22 of Revelation and 1 & 2 of Genesis give us a picture of what life looks like in a perfect, sinless world.

For this reason, mankind desperately needs a Savior. Those who abused you are responsible for their sinful choices and they will answer to a righteous Judge—God—one day, according to Galatians 6:7-8: **"Do not be deceived: God is not mocked, for whatever one sows, that will he also reap. For the one who sows to his own flesh will from the flesh reap corruption, but the one who sows to the Spirit will from the Spirit reap eternal life."** Your abusers (and everyone) will stand before God and give an account for their sinful choices against you because those sinful choices are ultimately against a Holy God who is angry about their sin.

One attribute of God that is difficult to understand for those who have been abused is that God is long-suffering, or patient, even with the wicked. Look at the description that God gives of Himself as He passes by Moses in Exodus 34:6: **"The Lord passed before him and proclaimed, "The Lord, the Lord, a God merciful and gracious, slow to anger, and abounding in steadfast love and faithfulness, keeping steadfast love for thousands, forgiving iniquity and transgression and sin, but who will by no means clear the guilty, visiting the iniquity of the fathers on the children and the children's children, to the third and the fourth generation."** God is "slow to anger … forgiving iniquity and transgression and sin, but who will by no means clear the guilty," meaning that He does not allow sinful choices to go without consequences.

Will you ever see justice on this earth? Maybe, but maybe not. It is not for you to decide. As someone who has been abused, here is what you must do. First of all, you must pray for your abusers. Ask God to forgive them. Ask God to give you a forgiving attitude toward them.

Another action you must pray about taking is more difficult. If your abuser has never repented nor asked for your forgiveness, you should pray about how to approach this person about their sin out of concern for their eternal welfare. You should never do this alone! So why should you say something to them? Because their eternal destination may be hell and you may be called upon to call for their repentance.

In the Old Testament, God sent His prophets to call out to His people Israel to repent of their sins and to turn back to Him. God may want you to do the same thing in a letter, email, or face-to-face meeting. If this is not possible due to death or separation or other circumstances, then the answer is clear that you do not have to do this.

However, if this person is available and if you have prayed and asked God to make it clear, then you should consider contacting the person who sinned against you. Do this with considerable prayer and with someone to go with you. If you decide to write a letter, ask someone to help you write it, proofread it, and possibly to sign it with you. Never do this alone!

Your purpose for confronting the person must be out of love and deep concern for the destination of their soul. It is speaking the truth in love (Ephesians 4:15) and it is a very hard thing to do. It must be saturated with gracious words and conveyed in the right spirit. The person who sinned against you will respond in one of two ways: (1) repentant or (2) not repentant.

If the person is repentant, then praise the Lord! If the person is not repentant, then you will know that you have obeyed the Lord and done your part. There is nothing more you can do outside of continuing to pray for their repentance. The person is in the Lord's Hands and is making his or her own choice. God grants repentance (Romans 2:4 and 2 Timothy 2:25), so it is up to Him to bring about a change of heart and mind leading to a change in actions in the person who harmed you.

Regardless of the outcome, your response is to be like Christ, who was brutally abused by unbelievers and abandoned by those closest to Him. He was left all alone and it was not because of His own sin but the sin of others. Likewise, the abuse you experienced was not the result of your own sinful choice but the sinful choices of others. How you choose to respond is the key. Respond in love and with love toward your offender, who is lost and does not know what he or she is doing. They will be held accountable to a righteous Judge one day soon; be assured that at that moment of judgment, the abuser will know what he or she did and the person will then reap what they have sown.

We live in a fallen world, cursed due to mankind's sin in Genesis 3. God wants you to be a peace-maker who is used by Him to reconcile lost souls to Himself (Matthew 5:9). Christians are to live at peace with others, even those who have spitefully used them, according to Matthew 5:11-12: **"Blessed are you when others revile you and persecute you and utter all kinds of evil against you falsely on my account. Rejoice and be glad, for your reward is great in heaven, for so they persecuted the prophets who were before you."** In Matthew 5:43-45, Jesus takes His teaching further: **"You have heard that it was said, 'You shall love your neighbor and hate your enemy.' But I say to you, Love your enemies and pray for those who persecute you, so that you may be sons of your Father who is in heaven. For he makes his sun rise on the evil and on the good, and sends rain on the just and on the unjust."** Nowhere in Jesus' teachings are we encouraged to retaliate with evil toward our enemies.

The Bible even commands you NOT to be overcome by evil. In other words, you cannot be defeated by the abuse you have experienced. That abuse does not define who you are—unless you allow it to do so. You no longer have to live and think like a victim; you can choose to respond with righteous actions. Romans 12:21 commands you: **"Do not be overcome by evil, but overcome evil with good."** When you pray for your abuser or confront him by speaking the truth in love, you are overcoming evil with good no matter what the abuser's response may be.

Think about this: if your abuser becomes a true Christian, then you will have watched the Lord save a soul from hell and you will have prevented future abuse from occurring. It is a win-win situation that only God can do. But God does so through willing vessels like you and me.

Finally, live by Jesus' words in Luke 17:3-4: **"Pay attention to yourselves! If your brother sins, rebuke him, and if he repents, forgive him, and if he sins against you seven times in the day, and turns to you seven times, saying, 'I repent,' you must forgive him."** Speak up when you are offended by others, but do so primarily for their benefit, not your own. If they repent, then take them at their word and forgive them. This may not mean that you will ever be very close to them again. Forgiving them is not saying you will automatically become best friends since that may never happen. However, forgiveness does show them the love of Christ and obeys God's commands in Ephesians 4:32: **"Be kind to one another, tenderhearted, forgiving one another, as God in Christ forgave you."**

Appendix F
Meditation and Controlling Our Thoughts

Be aware of a common misunderstanding about meditation and the ability to control your thoughts. In the Eastern world, meditation is commonly thought to be a time of centering your thoughts upon yourself or just letting go of control by letting your mind wander. Many think this type of Eastern meditation is a time when a "higher power" speaks to you. However, biblical meditation is intentional. It is focused upon the Word of God since God has already spoken to us through His Son and His Holy Word.

When you meditate biblically, focus your thoughts on the Word of God and His work in your life. Memorize, repeat, and saturate yourself in a particular passage of Scripture and apply it to your heart. Likewise, when you are battling your thoughts, do not allow your mind to wander and think whatever you want to think. Instead, focus your thoughts on what is pure (Philippians 4:8) and direct your thoughts to Christ-like things that are true and good.

You must plan ahead in anticipation of the temptations you will face in overcoming a physical addiction. One practical tool that can help you is a "think list" or "gratitude list." When preparing a gratitude list, there are two verses from the Bible that are really helpful. Philippians 4:8-9 states:

> **Finally, brothers, whatever is true, whatever is honorable, whatever is just, whatever is pure, whatever is lovely, whatever is commendable, if there is any excellence, if there is anything worthy of praise, think about these things. What you have learned and received and heard and seen in me— practice these things, and the God of peace will be with you.**

Utilize verse 8 to help you develop a list of those things that are true, honorable, just, pure, lovely, commendable, excellent, and worthy of praise, for which you can be grateful. Then, follow the verse 9 command to practice these things by reading this list aloud every morning to start your day and throughout the day when you are tempted to feed your "perishing mentality." Make multiple copies of it to keep in your pocket, in your car, in your nightstand, in your Bible, and anywhere else for quick access.

We have discussed the progression of "mentalities" that lead to addictive thinking. You need to be proactive in your thinking to prevent relapse. The "victim" and "perishing" mentalities are perhaps the most dangerous for you and must be resisted to avoid giving in to addictive choices. Being proactive means controlling your thoughts through biblical meditation.

Take a sheet of paper, turn it sideways, and create a chart like the one below to help you visualize how to make a gratitude list so that you can create your own!

True	Honorable	Just	Pure	Lovely	Commendable	Excellent	Praiseworthy

Also, below is a list of verses you can meditate upon to help cultivate a thankful heart. Spend time thinking about one verse per day or week. Meditate upon it and try to memorize it. You will be able to memorize it as you "practice" it more and more. Then, you will have a powerful weapon to use against the lies of the enemy and the attacks on your values that come from the world. This is not a comprehensive list as there are many, many more passages of thankfulness in the Bible. Take the time and find other Scriptures that remind you of how good God is and how thankful we should be.

Therefore let us be grateful for receiving a kingdom that cannot be shaken, and thus let us offer to God acceptable worship, with reverence and awe, for our God is a consuming fire (Hebrews 12:28-29).

Through him then let us continually offer up a sacrifice of praise to God, that is, the fruit of lips that acknowledge his name (Hebrews 13:15).

I will give to the Lord the thanks due to his righteousness, and I will sing praise to the name of the Lord, the Most High (Psalm 7:17).

Oh give thanks to the Lord, for he is good, for his steadfast love endures forever! Let the redeemed of the Lord say so, whom he has redeemed from trouble (Psalm 107:1-2).

Oh give thanks to the Lord; call upon his name; make known his deeds among the peoples! Sing to him, sing praises to him; tell of all his wondrous works! Glory in his holy name; let the hearts of those who seek the Lord rejoice (Psalm 105:1-3).

And be thankful. Let the word of Christ dwell in you richly, teaching and admonishing one another in all wisdom, singing psalms and hymns and spiritual songs, with thankfulness in your hearts to God. And whatever you do, in word or deed, do everything in the name of the Lord Jesus, giving thanks to God the Father through him (Colossians 3:15b-17)

Therefore, as you received Christ Jesus the Lord, so walk in him, rooted and built up in him and established in the faith, just as you were taught, abounding in thanksgiving (Colossians 2:6-7).

I will give thanks to the Lord with my whole heart; I will recount all of your wonderful deeds. I will be glad and exult in you; I will sing praise to your name, O Most High (Psalm 9:1-2).

Preserve me, O God, for in you I take refuge. I say to the Lord, "You are my Lord; I have no good apart from you" (Psalm 16:1-2).

Therefore my heart is glad, and my whole being rejoices; my flesh also dwells secure (Psalm 16:9).

Who delivered me from my enemies; yes, you exalted me above those who rose against me; you rescued me from the man of violence (Psalm 18:48).

The Lord is my strength and my shield; in him my heart trusts, and I am helped; my heart exults, and with my song I give thanks to him (Psalm 28:7).

I will thank you forever, because you have done it. I will wait for your name, for it is good, in the presence of the godly (Psalm 52:9).

I will give thanks to you, O Lord, among the peoples; I will sing praises to you among the nations. For your steadfast love is great to the heavens, your faithfulness to the clouds (Psalm 57:9-10).

But we your people, the sheep of your pasture, will give thanks to you forever; from generation to generation we will recount your praise (Psalm 79:13).

Oh give thanks to the Lord, for he is good, for his steadfast love endures forever! (Psalm 107:1).

Let them thank the Lord for his steadfast love, for his wondrous works to the children of men! (Psalm 107:8).

Let them thank the Lord for his steadfast love, for his wondrous works to the children of men! (Psalm 107:15).

Let them thank the Lord for his steadfast love, for his wondrous works to the children of men! (Psalm 107:21).

Let them thank the Lord for his steadfast love, for his wondrous works to the children of men! (Psalm 107:31).

I will give thanks to you, O Lord, among the peoples; I will sing praises to you among the nations (Psalm 108:3).

Praise the Lord, all nations! Extol him, all peoples! For great is his steadfast love toward us, and the faithfulness of the Lord endures forever. Praise the Lord! (Psalm 117:1-2).

With my mouth I will give great thanks to the Lord; I will praise him in the midst of the throng (Psalm 109:30).

Oh give thanks to the Lord, for he is good; for his steadfast love endures forever! (Psalm 118:1).

I was glad when they said to me, "Let us go to the house of the Lord!" (Psalm 122:1).

Praise the Lord! Praise the name of the Lord, give praise, O servants of the Lord, who stand in the house of the Lord, in the courts of the house of our God! Praise the Lord, for the Lord is good; sing to his name, for it is pleasant! For the Lord has chosen Jacob for himself, Israel as his own possession. For I know that the Lord is great, and that our Lord is above all gods. Whatever the Lord pleases, he does, in heaven and on earth, in the seas and all deeps. He it is who makes the clouds rise at the end of the earth, who makes lightnings for the rain and brings forth the wind from his storehouses (Psalm 135:1-7).

Give thanks to the Lord, for he is good, for his steadfast love endures forever. Give thanks to the God of gods, for his steadfast love endures forever. Give thanks to the Lord of lords, for his steadfast love endures forever (Psalm 136:1-3).

I give you thanks, O Lord, with my whole heart; before the gods I sing your praise; I bow down toward your holy temple and give thanks to your name for your steadfast love and your faithfulness, for you have exalted above all things your name and your word. On the day I called, you answered me; my strength of soul you increased. All the kings of the earth shall give you thanks, O Lord, for they have heard the words of your mouth, and they shall sing of the ways of the Lord, for great is the glory of the Lord. For though the Lord is high, he regards the lowly, but the haughty he knows from afar. Though I walk in the midst of trouble, you preserve my life; you stretch out your hand against the wrath of my enemies, and your right hand delivers me. The Lord will fulfill his purpose for me; your steadfast love, O Lord, endures forever. Do not forsake the work of your hands (Psalm 138:1-8).

Praise the Lord! Praise God in his sanctuary; praise him in his mighty heavens! Praise him for his mighty deeds; praise him according to his excellent greatness! Praise him with trumpet sound; praise him with lute and harp! Praise him with tambourine and dance; praise him with strings and pipe! Praise him with sounding cymbals; praise him with loud clashing cymbals! Let everything that has breath praise the Lord! Praise the Lord! (Psalm 150:1-6).

... saying, "We give thanks to you, Lord God Almighty, who is and who was, for you have taken your great power and begun to reign" (Revelation 11:17).

And they were to stand every morning, thanking and praising the Lord, and likewise at evening (1 Chronicles 23:30).

You may wonder why I conclude with the following verse. I included it as a warning—a warning to those who refuse to honor God as God or give thanks to Him!

For although they knew God, they did not honor him as God or give thanks to him, but they became futile in their thinking, and their foolish hearts were darkened (Romans 1:21).

Appendix G
For Further Study

Many people using this workbook may also be meeting with a biblical counselor. If so, then the following questions are designed for further study on this issue. Use a separate notebook, journal, or paper to complete the following assignments:

1. List 5 people you can call the second you get an urge or craving to relapse.

2. What are 5 things you can think about to replace your thoughts when you get a craving? Read Philippians 4:8 and use that verse to help you develop your list of things to think on.

3. Begin journaling the events, thoughts, and feelings you experience during the day. Write down places, people, and things you see that may tempt you to relapse. Be specific.

4. Write down 3 positive events or testimonies where you saw God's faithfulness in your life.

5. Write down 3 times where you witnessed God's wisdom in a practical way in your life.

6. Read, write, and memorize Ephesians 5:18-21.

7. Read Proverbs 23:29-35. How did you compare to this proverb when you were involved actively in your addiction? Be detailed and specific.

8. Write out a prayer to God based upon Psalm 23 or another psalm. Insert your name into that passage of Scripture.

9. Read Psalm 139. What does this psalm tell you about God?

10. Read Psalm 1 and identify persons, situations, places, and things that compare with this psalm in your own personal life story.

11. Make a weekly plan to exercise and eat healthy, well-balanced meals and then implement it.

12. Make a plan and implement it to go to bed earlier and to wake up earlier each day (1 Thessalonians 5:17: **"For those who sleep, sleep at night, and those who get drunk, are drunk at night."**)

13. Enlist the help of 3 prayer partners to focus their prayers on your situation for two weeks. Ask for God's will to be done and for you to be accepting of His sovereign decisions.

14. Eliminate the word "my" and "mine" from your vocabulary for one week. Do not use any possessive pronoun so that you are reminded that everything belongs to God and you are only His steward (or manager) of His things.

15. Replace the word "need" with either "want" or "desire" when you are tempted to misuse "need." For example, "I need a soft drink" should be replaced with "I want a soft drink." Also, "I need new clothes" can be replaced with "I desire new clothes."

16. Assess your willingness honestly. Are you willing to glorify and please God more than you want to breathe? Write out a short journal entry on your willingness or lack of willingness.

17. Understand that manipulation is simply a deceitful attempt to control a situation. How have you manipulated others when trying to get what you wanted? List 3 examples.

18. How have you lied in the past in order to relapse? How can you utilize Ephesians 4:25 to overcome lying? What does God think of a lying tongue according to Proverbs 6:16-19? What else does God hate according to Proverbs 6:16-19 and have you been guilty of such sins?

19. Analyze your relationships with at least 10 of your closest friends and relatives. With whom do you need to ask forgiveness? With whom do you need to pay restitution? Write an honest letter to each of them confessing your sin, acknowledging the hurt you caused, asking for forgiveness, and asking them how you might repent and repay them for what you have done?

20. Write down as many words as you can to describe what life was like when you were in active addiction. Then, write down as many words as you can to describe what life is like now (or will be like soon) in your process of transformation.

21. What age did you first try alcohol or other drugs? How old are you now? Subtract your age now (or when you last used a drug or alcohol) from the age you first tried a drug. That is how many years alcohol and other drugs have been a part of your life. Ask God to redeem the days you lost by His grace and mercy.

22. What is your addictive pleasure (or drug) of choice? In other words, if you could choose any addictive pleasure in the world, what would it be? When was the last time you used your drug of choice? Use this date to help encourage you as a start date for a new life of sobriety and surrender to Christ.

23. How can you become a better employee at your job now that your addictive pleasure is no longer consuming you?

24. Read Exodus 20:3. How have you violated this first commandment in relation to your addictive pleasure of choice?

25. Read Exodus 20:3-17. How have you violated these ten commandments, even if just in your thought life since sin can also be committed in one's mind (Matthew 5:28)? How has God forgiven you from these sins and how is/can He redeem you from these sins by giving you new ways to live as replacements for these sin?

26. How have you sinned by omission? In other words, what did you FAIL to do that God called you to do? For example, did you fail to pray, trust God, read your Bible, honor your spouse, love your spouse, care for your children, respect your parents, be a faithful employee, etc.? Then, how can God restore and forgive you so that you can now do these things more faithfully and regularly? What is your plan to do your part to obey God in these areas?

27. Read Psalm 106:36 and Psalm 115:4-8 about idols. What do these verses say about you if you continue to pursue an idolatrous desire for your addictive pleasure of choice?

28. Read Isaiah 44:9-20. What do these verses tell you about the foolishness of idolatry? Be specific and list at least 10 things. How have you personally been fooled by your idols in the past?

29. Read Psalm 19. What does this psalm tell you about God? Write down at least 7 things.

30. Read Proverb 23:19-21. What happens to gluttons and drunkards?

31. Read Genesis 9:20-27 and Genesis 19:30-38. How did these one-time events of drunkenness affect entire families and generations of people?

32. List 10 warning signs, temptations, or "triggers" that might lead you to a relapse. How can you plan to overcome these with godly choices? Be practical and specific.

33. Read 1 Corinthians 13:4-8. Write the characteristics of love and put your name beside each one with an honest evaluation from 1 to 10 of how you reflect each attribute. For example, "Love is patient. (6) I am not patient with my wife and children." Did you realize that If you are not a patient person, then you are unloving according to this passage of Scripture? How can you be more patient in the future to demonstrate love to others?

34. Make a list of things you can do to love others without anyone knowing and do some of them.

35. According to the Bible, who is God (Exodus 34:6-7; Psalm 139; Romans 1:18-20)? In other words, describe His attributes and character using these verses and others you may know?

36. According to the Bible, who is mankind (Genesis 5:3; Romans 1-3; Romans 3:23; Romans 6:23)? Are people good people who make bad decisions or sinners in need of God's saving grace? Explain in detail using Scriptures.

37. According to the Bible, who is Christ (Matthew 16:16; John 1:1-4 & 14; Hebrews 1:3; Ephesians 1:7; Titus 2:14; Romans 3:25; Romans 5:10-11; Romans 8:33-34; 2 Corinthians 5:21)? Use Scriptures listed to explain.

38. According to the Bible, what is faith (Romans 1:17, 3:20-21, 4:22-25, 10:9-10)? Use Scriptures.

39. According to the Bible, what is eternity (Daniel 12:1-2; Acts 4:12; Acts 17:30-31; 1 John 5:12)? What two destinations are awaiting all people according to Jesus in Matthew 25:46? Which destination will be your eternal home after you die? Explain using Scripture.

Appendix H
Additional Resources

This appendix is written to help you find other helpful resources to use as part of your relapse program.

Mark Shaw's Resources

The Heart of Addiction is a resource that addresses any type of "addiction" but especially drugs and alcohol. This book covers the subject of addiction in a comprehensive (though not exhaustive) and practical manner. The book is full of Scripture and is designed to teach biblical passages that go in-depth to address issues of the heart for people who struggle with addiction.

The Heart of Addiction Workbook is a relational book designed to be worked by the "addict" and reviewed by a trusted Christian friend (TCF). I want the addict to do the work but not alone. It is best for the addict to be discipled by someone more mature in Christ who will utilize the workbook to launch into a variety of intimate topics related to addiction. Again, this is a relational, counseling tool when used at its best but many small groups use this workbook in discussion groups as well.

Addiction-Proof Parenting is a prevention book written for parents specifically, but has broader principles that apply to any person. This book explains addictive thinking and how to replace that mindset with the mind of Christ. Anyone can benefit from reading and *doing* this book.

Cross Talking: A Daily Gospel is a 45 day devotional that reinforces biblical principles of addiction. Sometimes, we utilize this book as a group and read one or two days to discuss as a group.

Divine Intervention: Hope and Help for Families of Addicts is a book written to family members of those who struggle with addiction. While not written directly to the addict, this book can be helpful to an addict to understand how selfish a person can become when in active addiction. This book will help family and friends of an addict and will challenge them to make hard, loving decisions as an act of faith in God.

Hope and Help for Videogame, TV, and Internet "Addiction" is a booklet designed to help people understand the basic approach of the Bible in helping us to overcome any type of "addiction."

Hope and Help for Self-Injurers and Cutters is a booklet specifically written to those who are ensnared in the trap of injuring themselves. The booklet demonstrates that this is not a new problem but a problem that the Word of God addresses and is sufficient to help a person to overcome through the power of the Holy Spirit.

Hope and Help for Gambling is a booklet written to convict and encourage those battling this particular "addiction." Sometimes, I have counselees read it so that they better understand what it means to be a good steward of God's resources bestowed upon them.

Resources Critiquing the Disease Concept and 12 Step Theory of Addiction

The Useful Lie is an excellent book that exposes the lies about the "disease model" of addiction and presents God's truth about this problem as a sin problem. I highly recommend this book for anyone struggling with whether or not addiction is a sin. Written by Dr. William L. Playfair, M.D.

Resources for Drugs and Alcohol

Where Sin Abounds Does Grace Abound More? is a book that presents a personal testimony and then a biblical approach to overcome addiction. There is a wealth of information in this book written by the late Don Bowen.

Addictions: A Banquet in the Grave written by Dr. Edward T. Welch is a comprehensive, theological approach for overcoming addiction. This is a book that is packed with biblical truth that will impact your life. Dr. Welch has many books that are helpful for overcoming an addiction.

NOTE: A quote from Dr. Howard Eyrich: **"Ed Welch gives us the theological and theoretical framework for a biblical approach to addictions. Mark Shaw gives us the practical implementation and motivational energy for biblically counseling the addict."**

Resources for Sexual Addiction

A Biblical Guide to Counseling the Sexual Addict by Steve Gallagher is a systematic, structured guide for setting up a support group for those who struggle with sexual addiction. His book, *At the Altar of Sexual Idolatry* examines sexual sin and provides biblical solutions.

General Resources

Idols of the Heart: Learning to Long for God Alone by Elyse Fitzpatrick is a book that helps a person to diagnose the sinful desires of the heart so that the power of the Holy Spirit can transform the desires of the heart.

From Pride to Humility by Dr. Stuart Scott is a power-packed booklet that we use to help people to see what pride looks like in their own hearts and what humility looks like when produced by the Holy Spirit. This is an essential booklet to use with anyone struggling with any type of addiction. (Focus Publishing)

The Gospel Primer by Milton Vincent is a short, thorough presentation of the biblical gospel. Addicts must understand who God is, who they are (sinners), and who Christ is and this book will help them tremendously. (Focus Publishing)